HOME THEATER
SOLUTIONS

Joel White

Home Theater Solutions

Shown on cover (clockwise from top right): 57" Toshiba 16x9 HDTV; Onkyo TX-DS595 A/V Receiver; Onkyo CHAD LCD remote control; Aperion Audio speakers and subwoofer.

Credits: Senior Editor, Mark Garvey; Production Editor, Rodney A. Wilson; Development Editor, Don Prues; Copyeditor, Karen Annett; Technical Editor, Jake Pratt; Cover Design and Interior Design and Layout, Chad Planner, Pop Design Works; Indexer, Melody Englund, Songbird Indexing.

Publisher: Andy Shafran

MUSKA&LIPMAN

Library of Congress Catalog Number: 2002112964

ISBN 1-929685-67-X

5   4   3   2   1

Educational facilities, companies, and organizations interested in multiple copies or licensing of this book should contact the publisher for quantity discount information. Training manuals, CD-ROMs, and portions of this book are also available individually or can be tailored for specific needs.

Muska & Lipman Publishing
2645 Erie Avenue, Suite 41
Cincinnati, Ohio 45208
www.muskalipman.com
publisher@muskalipman.com

About the Author

Joel White is the founder and editor of CheapHomeTheater.com, a website that independently reviews home theater components. He works for a software company that develops software for the oil and gas industry and lives with his family in Tulsa, Oklahoma.

Dedication

To Jill for helping me get through the tight deadlines, tough times, and for keeping our two dogs, Baloo and Molly, in check while I worked.

Acknowledgments

I would like to thank my wife Jill for her support. Thanks to Jake Pratt and Bryan Davis for helping me come up with the idea for the website and helping me along the way. Thanks to Don Prues and Mark Garvey for turning my random thoughts into something readable. I would also like to thank Sherri Schwartz and Kathy O'Hara for their contributions. Also thanks to Jake Pratt, Bryan and Cindy Davis, Jason and Jennifer Brandt, and Anup Chackunny for letting me intrude on their lives to take pictures of their home theater systems.

Contents

Introduction

If you're reading this book, chances are you're a movie lover. And that means you're used to going to the theater to enjoy great movies. But it also probably means that you've grown a little tired of all the hassles that are involved with the theater-going experience: driving to the theater, worrying about parking, finding a good seat (and craning your neck or squinting your eyes if you don't), listening to noisy teens talking or popcorn eaters crunching, and, of course, paying the ever-escalating prices for admission tickets.

No doubt you would like to enjoy the movie-theater experience in your own home, without the aforementioned drawbacks, which is probably why you picked up this book to begin with. I'm sure you've contemplated the idea of creating your dream home theater system, and now you're ready to turn those mere wonderings into actualities. Congratulations—you're making a wise choice.

Interest in home theater has been gaining momentum in the past few years and it shows no signs of slowing down. With rapid developments in technology and a growing number of enthusiasts purchasing the latest equipment, the biggest beneficiary in home theater is the budget-minded consumer. Although it used to take thousands of dollars to obtain big, movie theater-like sound, these days it's not so difficult. In fact, a smart-shopping budget consumer (you!) can achieve a great-sounding home theater system for much, much less than was previously possible. It really is possible to obtain an awesome home theater experience while not breaking your bank.

In the end, though, it doesn't really matter how much you spend on your home theater system. What counts is how much you enjoy it. With some thought, careful selection, and the help of Home Theater Solutions, you'll build a great system you can enjoy fully. Before long, you'll find yourself waiting for theatrical releases to wrap up their stay in first-run theaters so they can make their way to DVD, which is when you can watch them in the comfort and privacy of your own home—without waiting in ticket lines, fighting crowds, or paying exorbitant admission prices.

What You'll Find in This Book

Home Theater Solutions provides you with:

- ▶ Instructions on how to identify, select, and set up the necessary equipment for your home theater system
- ▶ Hands-on examples with illustrations that show you how to work with your system, from connecting speakers to programming your remote control
- ▶ In-depth knowledge on the components, surround sound formats, and video technology that make up a home theater system
- ▶ Guides for establishing a budget, sticking with it, and maximizing your dollars to obtain the best home theater experience possible

- Cost-effective solutions to typical home theater problems, from steadying a shaky subwoofer to selecting a capable-but-affordable universal remote control
- Advice on how to distinguish home theater technology facts from marketing propaganda. Do you really need to buy a component that's THX certified?
- Recommendations on how to achieve the best sound and video from your system
- Techniques that break down the sometimes daunting task of building a complete system from scratch (we carve it into small, simple, easy-to-follow bits)
- Descriptions of home theater system components and their functions
- Real-world home theater systems that not only offer you a little inspiration, but also practical pointers on how to make the most out of quirky room arrangements

Who This Book is For

Unfortunately for most of us, the grand home theater ideas we dream about tend to exceed our meager budgets. But that doesn't mean you can't create a capable, enjoyable home theater system. You can, and I'm going to show you how. Let's face it: Home theater systems aren't cheap. But they can be within your reach, especially if you know how much you plan to spend, what you need for your system, and what you can do without. This book will help you build the best home theater system possible for your dollars.

This book is for you if:

- You've ever considered building a home theater
- You feel overwhelmed by the thought of owning and setting up a home theater system
- You want to build a great home theater but must do so on a shoestring budget
- You love movies but are tired of all the hassles involved with going to the theater
- You're torn about whether to emphasize the audio or video aspect of your home theater
- You want to become an informed home theater enthusiast who makes wise buying decisions
- You want to know about the best websites, manufacturers, and online retailers in the home theater industry
- You are dead set on getting the best components for your money
- You at one time opted for a Home Theater in a Box solution but now are ready to upgrade—on a budget, of course
- You've built a home theater system but are looking to get better sound and video out of it

How This Book is Organized

This book contains eleven chapters, two appendices, and a glossary. Now let's take a look at the contents of each.

▶ Chapter 1: "The Home Theater Difference." This chapter offers you an overview of home theater and its technologies. You'll be introduced to the many home theater components and offered tips for making the most of your system.

▶ Chapter 2: "Surround Sound Formats." We walk you through the various surround sound formats and explain the differences of each. We evaluate why some surround sound formats work better in some situations than others. You may realize that you want to go with cutting-edge technologies, such as Dolby Digital EX or DTS ES, or you may come to the decision that your current room setup or budget mandates a typical 5.1 digital surround system. This chapter helps you figure out what format is best for you. We discuss the three primary audio formats.

▶ Chapter 3: "Home Theater Audio Components." You'll be initiated into the mighty world of home theater audio components, such as receivers, amplifiers, and separates. We show you how to evaluate these components to ensure you get the sound that fits your needs. You'll also be introduced to the different types of speakers in a home theater system, such as bookshelf speakers, bipolar speakers, and powered subwoofers.

▶ Chapter 4: "Home Theater Video Components." This chapter sheds light on the video components commonly found in home theater systems. The various types of television sets and video monitors are explored, as well as some alternatives for video display (such as projectors). In addition, we cover personal video recorders (PVRs) and VCRs.

▶ Chapter 5: "Setting a Budget." This is where we help you establish a budget for your system. You'll learn how to appropriately determine what you should spend on each aspect of your system, including specific components (all the way down to the cost of wires and cables). By establishing your priorities up front, you can allocate the funds in your budget properly.

▶ Chapter 6: "Selecting the Right Equipment." You'll be shown how to intelligently discern which home theater components you need. Do you want your system geared toward audio or video? What can you do to make sure you don't shortchange one aspect of your system in favor of the other?

▶ Chapter 7: "Shopping for Your System." In this chapter, we explore not what to buy but where and from whom to buy it. The options for shopping for home theater components are many, and we walk you through these, from buying on the Internet from direct-to-consumer manufacturers to buying from your local merchants. This chapter also explores common questions, such as "Should all my components be the same brand?" and "Is it okay to buy refurbished items?"

▶ Chapter 8: "Connecting All the Components." We show you how to master the most feared aspect of assembling a home theater system—hooking up the various components. We demystify this connection process by breaking it down into easy-to-follow steps. You'll learn about the different types of cables and connections, and we show you how to create a wiring diagram. It won't take long for you to quickly and easily identify the type and length of cables you need for each connection.

▶ Chapter 9: "Getting the Most Out of Your Home Theater." We explore how to obtain the maximum performance out of your system. This chapter introduces you to decibel meters and calibration discs, and shows you how to properly tune the audio and video aspects of your home theater system. We also consider the ins and outs of spending money on having your system professionally calibrated.

▶ Chapter 10: "Using Your System." This chapter shows you how to use your system and gives you ideas on how to make your system easy to operate. You'll learn how to program your remote to control your entire system, including how to make use of its advanced features, such as its macro-creation and learning abilities. We also discuss using your receiver's video-switching capability, managing your cables, and selecting the best audio format for the given situation.

▶ Chapter 11: "The Upgrade Path." This chapter is devoted to helping you maximize your upgrade dollars. You'll learn how to identify which components are most likely to need upgrading first. We also tap into how you can use your old components instead of tossing them in the trash. And we go over things you might want to consider if you plan on moving from a budget to a high-end system.

▶ Appendix A: "Web Yellow Pages of Useful Home Theater Sites." If you need go to the web to find out more information than what's provided in this book, this chapter points you in the right direction. We've assembled a detailed appendix here, with the best product review sites, home theater forums, audio and video manufacturer sites, and online retailer sites. By consulting Appendix A, you'll learn where to go on the web for all your home theater needs.

▶ Appendix B: "Real World Home Theater Examples." Have you wondered how you might make the most of the quirks in your home theater room? Have you wondered how others have made the most of their less-than-optimal rooms (with three-walled rooms, hardwood floors, and windows galore)? Read Appendix B to see and learn how everyday budget enthusiasts have set up their theaters, including what components they use and why. This appendix is a great idea generator for you, the home theater owner.

▶ Appendix C: "Glossary." The most commonly used terms in home theater are defined here, from anamorphic wide-screen and coaxial cable to Dolby Pro Logic II.

1

The Home Theater Difference

Nothing beats going to the movie theater to see the new action movie that overloads your senses with amazing sights and even more incredible sounds. Of course, the teenager sitting right next to you keeps talking on his cell phone, a baby is crying behind you, and there's a puddle of sticky substance under your feet. Is it really worth subjecting yourself—and your movie-going experience—to this, especially when you're paying ten dollars per ticket to watch the film? Didn't think so. It is easy to see why more and more people are bringing the theater experience to their own homes.

Moving Up to Home Theater

Home theater re-creates a personal cinema for your own viewing pleasure. The essence of home theater is forgetting you are sitting comfortably in your living room and instead believing you are part of the movie. Although you aren't likely to replicate the size and magnitude of the movie theater in your home, you can simulate it, especially the great sights and sounds.

Movie Theater Sound in Your Home

Home theater may often be confused with just having a huge television monitor to watch the game on, but even a system built around a small TV can deliver an incredible movie-watching experience. Try watching a movie on a large-screen television with sound only from the television itself compared to watching a smaller television monitor combined with a great home theater sound system. Most people agree that sound makes the difference. You probably won't be able to afford a television that allows you to re-create the visual aspect of a home theater to lifelike proportions; however, you can certainly create a home theater sound system that will immerse you with a true-to-life experience.

One Step at a Time

Although theater-quality sound in your own home probably sounds appealing, it may be a daunting task to purchase and set up your own home theater. Home Theater Solutions is here to help, by taking you step-by-step through the process. Through easy-to-follow steps, we help you identify what equipment you need, teach you how to hook it all up, and offer some money-saving tips and tweaks to maximize your home theater sound.

More Than Just Movies

You might think a home theater system is primarily for watching DVD movies at home, but that isn't all a home theater system can be used for. Sporting events, music listening, and even TV shows take on a new life when processed through a home theater system. Today, with digital music formats such as MP3s, it's easy to create a home jukebox that supplies hundreds of hours of great-sounding music. Video games also explode off the TV screen with realistic audio reproduction, adding a whole new level of realism. Home theater systems greatly increase your satisfaction with all aspects of TV watching.

Leverage What You Already Own

If you were to pick up a home theater magazine, you'd probably think it takes $25,000 to build a decent home theater. You might be surprised to find that your existing TV, VCR, satellite receiver, and DVD player can be leveraged into your new home theater system. With rising ticket costs at the movies, you might be able to buy that movie you want to see for less than it would cost to take the whole family to the theater.

Establishing and Sticking to a Budget

Many people have the misconception that home theater systems have to be extravagant and expensive. Not so. Home Theater Solutions helps you establish a budget and maximize your home theater dollars. This book covers all the areas of home theater and lets you know what components not to skimp on and what components you may be able to cut corners on. Also, we ensure you budget for the little things, such as cables and speaker stands, which can often push you over your preset budget.

Home Theater Components

A basic home theater system might consist of a television, home theater receiver, a DVD player, and speakers. The number and magnitude of speakers will certainly vary by budget, but most home theater systems consist of five separate speakers and a powered subwoofer (called a 5.1 setup). Of course, the more of these components you already own, the easier it is to convert these existing elements into a full home theater system.

The Receiver—the Center of Your Home Theater

Each of the components previously listed plays a vital role in turning your living room into a theater room. The home theater receiver (Figure 1.1) can be thought of as the brains and brawn—the central hub—of your home theater system. It provides the necessary decoding of various sound formats, and also provides the necessary amplification to reach realistic sound levels in your home. It also enables you to switch the audio and video between multiple sources. For instance, you can connect your satellite receiver (or cable box), a DVD player, and a VCR all into your home theater receiver and have your receiver control what audio and video are being reproduced.

Figure 1.1
A home theater receiver, here an Onkyo TX-DS595, is the center of your system

Let Your Speakers Do the Talking

A receiver can't do everything though, so speakers are also a necessity in your home theater. The number and size of the speakers will vary greatly due to budget, sound, and individual preference. Most budget home theaters consist of five speakers and a separately powered subwoofer as seen in the following illustration.

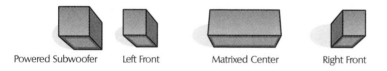

Powered Subwoofer   Left Front   Matrixed Center   Right Front

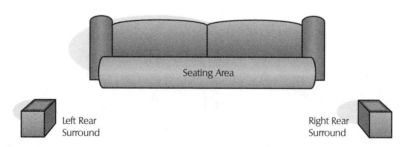

Seating Area

Left Rear
Surround

Right Rear
Surround

The five speakers consist of a left front, right front, a center channel, and two surround speakers behind or to the side of the listening area. The powered subwoofer, which re-creates the low frequency sounds that shake the walls, is usually placed in a corner of the room out of site. The receiver feeds a signal to each of the speakers, which then provides sound that fills the room. See a typical set of surround sound speakers in Figure 1.2.

Figure 1.2
A typical 5.1 surround sound speaker system consists of five satellite speakers and a subwoofer

Although speaker preference often varies per individual, Home Theater Solutions helps identify key characteristics to look for when shopping for home theater loudspeakers. We introduce you to concepts such as timbre matching, ensuring that the tonal characteristics of the speakers match.

Digital Picture and Sound

DVD players, now becoming a common household item, have always been an integral component in home theater systems. (See Figure 1.3.) In my opinion, the introduction of the digital surround formats has been the turning point in bringing true movie theater sound to a personal home theater. Dolby Digital and DTS surround formats bring home theater sound to a level comparable with giant screen movie theaters. The digital format not only brings great, dynamic sound, but also includes a digital picture that is clearly better than any other media currently available to consumers. A DVD player is certainly the most preferred way to demonstrate the dynamic sounds of your new home theater to your friends and family.

Figure 1.3
A DVD player, the Onkyo DV-S939, provides digital sound and picture to make movies come alive

Setting Up Your System

Home theater systems can be very intimidating with the vast amount of wires, cords, and remote controls. When broken up into components, the wiring and control of a home theater system can be greatly simplified. Most of the time, the receiver's remote control has learning ability. This allows the receiver remote to learn the codes from other remotes and allows you to take control of your entire home theater system with a single remote. A small investment of time up front to wire and set up your theater properly certainly pays off.

A tremendous home theater won't do you any good if you can't figure out how to use it. Home Theater Solutions shows you how to consolidate all the remotes scattered across your table into one remote that controls your entire system. By using the switching features built into your receiver, multiple inputs can be easily managed.

Making the Most of Your System

Budget systems and more extravagant systems benefit from basic tweaking techniques that help maximize the performance of the home theater setup. Tips and techniques are often simple and usually very cost effective. For instance, you can reduce interference by keeping speaker cables and power cables apart. Running these wires parallel to each other can frequently cause unwanted interference and diminish the overall performance of your home theater.

Every room has a different acoustical signature. This effect causes the same equipment to sound differently, for better or for worse, depending on the room it is placed in. An essential part of the home theater setup is a thorough and proper calibration of the audio and video system for the room in which they're being used. Using simple, cost-effective tools, such as a decibel meter and a calibration disc, you can greatly improve the performance of your home theater. Home Theater Solutions steps you through these money-saving processes to ensure you get top performance out of your home theater.

Enjoying the End Result

No home theater book is complete without some tips on which DVDs are "must haves" to show off your new home theater. We give our recommendations on DVDs that are certain to dazzle with glorious audio and visuals—certain to make you feel great about your new home theater.

Now that you've become familiar with the different components and steps necessary to build a great home theater system, we begin to explore these topics in a more detailed fashion.

2

Surround Sound Formats

To accurately re-create the movie theater experience at home, you need two things: a big screen and big sound. Although you won't be able to have a screen the same size as your local theater's, you can achieve a home theater sound that rivals the theater's. Because your living room is much smaller than the theater's viewing area, sound placement and imaging can be even more dramatic than in the theater. Although having a large video monitor is a big factor, home theater sound is the difference between watching a movie and experiencing it.

If you don't buy into the importance of home theater sound, try this experiment. Go to your local home theater retailer to demonstrate some of their gear. Try out some of their home theater systems. After you've watched a scene on a big screen with big sound, ask the salesman to turn off the home theater sound and just use the sound from the television. You'll quickly realize how much of the experience you've just lost. The sound makes you forget you are sitting comfortably at home and creates the illusion that you are part of the action.

Recorded sound has taken many steps since Edison's early success. From the phonograph, mono sound was then developed. Mono sound consisted of a single channel of sound that could reproduce an original recorded source. With the invention of stereo sound, two discrete channels of recorded sound allowed a recording to re-create location and provide imaging. Stereo sound is the building block that has allowed multichannel surround sound formats to progress to where they are today.

Most modern home theater systems have at least five full-range speakers and a dedicated low-frequency speaker. This basic home theater configuration is often referred to as "5.1." The five refers to the five speakers that are full-range speakers, meaning they reproduce all sounds in the audible spectrum. The ".1" is a distinction given to the low frequency effects channel that is used to re-create the low bass effects that are not only heard, but felt.

Choosing a Surround Sound Format

Surround sound, in the broadest sense of the definition, means being encompassed by sound. This can be accomplished with as few as two speakers and as many speakers as you can imagine. Typical home theater systems consist of between five and seven full-range speakers and a powered subwoofer, but the possibilities are bounded only by your space and budget. Surround sound physically surrounds the listening area and attempts to put you, the listener, in the center of the action. With speakers firing towards you from all directions, surround sound creates an environment that can easily make you believe you are experiencing the movie firsthand. When you have forgotten reality, surround sound has succeeded in its mission. When you watch a movie and look over your shoulder to see what that sound is behind you, you have truly realized what an integral part of the movie-watching experience surround sound is.

Surround sound is not a recent innovation. Movie theaters began using four-channel surround sound in the early 1950s as a way to enhance the movie-going experience. Films generally used several speakers across the front of the soundstage and at least one speaker in the rear of the theater. Filmmakers continued to try different methods to realistically create the illusion of three-dimensional sound, to create a realistic experience that captivated the audience.

Dolby Laboratories has been creating and developing surround sound for over twenty-five years. As with most technologies, surround sound has certainly seen dramatic technological improvements. In the beginning, Dolby Laboratories used a four-channel soundtrack that was encoded along with movies. This format, Dolby Surround, used an algorithm to develop four channels of surround sound information from a stereo (two-channel) source. Typically, these formats originate in the movie theaters, and make their way into consumer devices shortly thereafter.

Although surround sound was common in movie theaters, it wasn't until VHS players became commonplace that surround sound began to penetrate the home market. The earliest video cassette recorders featured only mono, single-channel soundtracks that left much to be desired. With the introduction of the Hi-fi VHS, consumers were introduced to stereo sound for home theater usage. Soon after the VHS gave consumers their first taste of higher fidelity sound, laserdisc players came along and showcased the possibilities of digital sound. Although the laserdisc failed to gain mainstream appeal, it did pave the way for digital video and digital surround sound.

There are true surround sound formats and also simulated surround sound formats. Your television may have a feature called simulated surround sound. This is an attempt to use acoustic effects to create a surround sound experience, but these simulated surround fields fall short. To achieve a feeling of being surrounded by the occurrences on the screen, speakers must physically be placed behind the listener. Two speakers in front of the listener simply cannot create a realistic surround field and a realistic experience for the listener. Often, these formats are more of a distraction than a benefit. If your television features a simulated surround sound, try listening to a sitcom. As soon as the laugh track is played, you'll hear the laughs emanating from the sides of your television, but in an unrealistic manner.

True surround formats consist of at least two speakers behind or to the side of the listener in addition to the speakers that are positioned in front of the listener. These formats create an expansive, realistic sound field. True surround sound formats have been around for some time, and you may be familiar with some of the more common formats, such as Dolby Pro Logic or Dolby Digital.

Dolby Pro Logic

Dolby Laboratories introduced Dolby Pro Logic surround encoding in 1987. Typically, Dolby Pro Logic can be found on VCR tapes and even normal broadcast television. This four-channel surround sound format revolutionized sound for the home consumer. This format uses a front left, front right, and front center channel, with a rear surround channel that plays a mono signal, as seen in Figure 2.1. The surround channel is a mono signal that plays the same sound in both the left and right rear speaker. This format began to be encoded in VHS tapes and television programs, providing the first real consumer home theater experience. The early adopters who had the home theater equipment capable of decoding the Pro Logic signal started to experience theater sound at home. See Figure 2.2.

Dolby Pro Logic combines the left and right channels to create a center channel. The single rear surround channel is also created by combining the left and right channels, but this time using the signal out of phase (similar to hooking up a speaker wire backwards). In addition the frequencies sent to the rear channel are limited to 110hz -7Khz. Channels that are created from combining two existing channels are known as matrixed channels. Dolby Pro Logic was certainly an effective surround format, but it also suffered from limitations. For instance, the rear surround channels are frequency limited. This means they cannot reproduce sounds that are outside their frequency range. Dolby Pro Logic also has no subwoofer channel to send low frequencies to a powered subwoofer, although some receivers can send low frequencies to a subwoofer if available. Also, as stated previously, the rear surround channel is mono, meaning both the left and right surround speakers play the exact same sounds.

Figure 2.1
A typical Dolby Pro Logic surround sound diagram

Left Front   Matrixed Center   Right Front

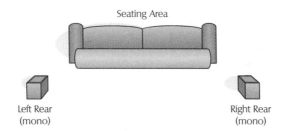

Seating Area

Left Rear
(mono)

Right Rear
(mono)

Dolby Pro Logic became the first home theater surround sound format to gain acceptance. Although this format was far from competing with a movie theater, it did create a more enjoyable experience than a simple stereo signal. VHS and television programming were given a new level of realism and increased entertainment value.

Figure 2.2
The Dolby Pro Logic logo lets you know that the media has been encoded with this surround sound format

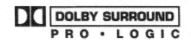

CHAPTER 2

Dolby Digital

Although the Pro Logic format certainly offered a new, exciting twist to watching movies, it still didn't hold a candle to the incredible sound at your local movie theater. Dolby Laboratories followed Dolby Pro Logic with an authentic digital surround format called Dolby Digital. Digital surround sound formats are far superior to their analog counterparts due to their ability to reproduce a cleaner, more accurate signal. Dolby Digital is the most common surround sound format found on DVD movies (see Figure 2.3). As the name implies, Dolby Digital is a true digital format consisting of five discrete, full-bandwidth channels and a dedicated, discrete, low-frequency channel. Dolby Digital is commonly referred to as 5.1 channel sound, due to its ability to provide five full discrete channels and a dedicated low frequency effects channel. It is sometimes also referred to as AC-3, derived from the Dolby multichannel encoding scheme that is used. Dolby Digital does not require all six channels but provides up to six.

The Dolby Digital format requires a massive amount of storage space. In fact, Dolby Digital requires almost three times as much storage space as a stereo signal. Even with the added storage space available on DVD media, a 5.1 channel soundtrack cannot fit on a DVD disc. To solve this problem, a compression algorithm is required to minimize the amount of storage space required for the digital soundtrack. Compression compacts the original recording, retaining roughly ten percent of the original source material and discards the rest. Upon playback, a reverse conversion is done that extracts the compressed data into a playable format. Dolby Digital uses a compression ratio of approximately 10:1. After compression, a movie and a 5.1 channel digital soundtrack can both fit on a DVD disc.

Figure 2.3
To be sure you are getting discrete digital surround sound, look for the Dolby Digital logo

Dolby Digital holds numerous advantages over the more limited Dolby Pro Logic surround format. The dedicated low-frequency channel, often called LFE, enables the use of a dedicated, powered subwoofer. Digital formats also provide much better reproduction of the original recording than their analog counterparts. Think of a compact disc versus a tape—a compact disc offers better sound. Unlike Dolby Pro Logic, Dolby Digital's rear surround channels are independent of each other. (See Figure 2.4.) They are also full bandwidth channels, which allow the reproduction of the entire range of frequencies that the human ear can hear. You may often see Dolby Digital referred to as a discrete format. This designation means the tracks are carried separately and are not matrixed, as in Dolby Pro Logic. Discretely carried channels sound noticeably better than matrixed channels.

Figure 2.4
A typical Dolby Digital home theater speaker configuration

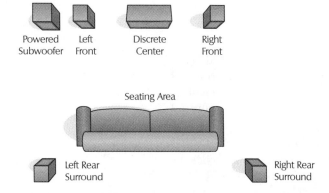

Dolby Digital is available on virtually every DVD today, and will be available on HDTV (high definition television) broadcasts in the near future. A recent trend is the inclusion of Dolby Digital soundtracks with today's newest video game consoles. The Microsoft Xbox features real-time Dolby Digital sound for many of its games. With 5.1 channels of discrete audio, the level of realism is greatly increased. For instance, when playing a car racing game, you hear competitors coming up behind you and you are able to distinguish from which side they are approaching.

DTS

DTS is a new and interesting digital format (see Figure 2.5). Very similar to Dolby Digital, DTS is a 5.1 channel digital surround format found on DVDs. Why bother with another format just like Dolby Digital? DTS uses less compression on the six channels of the soundtrack, which can produce a more accurate and slightly better-sounding reproduction. DTS uses a compression ratio of about 4:1. Many home theater users will not immediately notice a difference between Dolby Digital and DTS signals.

Figure 2.5
The DTS logo lets you know this item has support for this increasingly popular digital surround sound format

The Microsoft Xbox video console can also pass a DTS soundtrack to your home theater system. Just like Dolby Digital video game soundtracks, DTS soundtracks create a lifelike sound field that can easily make you forget that it's just a game.

CHAPTER 2

SELECTING DTS

Many DVDs feature DTS soundtracks, but you must go into the Audio Setup menu on the DVD and select the DTS soundtrack, as most discs default to Dolby surround. Almost all discs that feature a DTS soundtrack also have a Dolby Digital soundtrack included.

Dolby Pro Logic II

The newest surround format is an updated version of Dolby's Pro Logic format, appropriately named Dolby Pro Logic II, dubbed DPL II. DPL II is not a replacement for Dolby Digital, but is an upgrade to Dolby Pro Logic, making the listening material aurally crisper and more enjoyable. DPL II is similar to Dolby Pro Logic, as it creates a matrixed center channel from the left and right channel information. However, DPL II includes stereo rear surrounds. This means you hear different sounds out of the two rear channels. These rear channels are also full-bandwidth channels instead of the limited bandwidth surround channel in the original Dolby Pro Logic. Another major improvement is the inclusion of a dedicated low-frequency channel like Dolby Digital. See Figure 2.6.

Figure 2.6
A typical Dolby Pro Logic II surround sound system setup

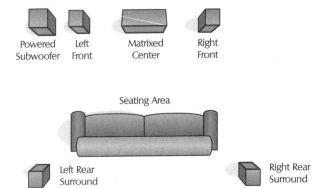

DPL II certainly breathes new life into broadcast television signals and VCR tapes (see Figure 2.7). DPL II is commonly divided into two subdivisions: Dolby Pro Logic II music and Dolby Pro Logic II movie. As the name implies, DPL II music mode creates an encompassing 5.1 channel surround field for your stereo music. Some receivers offer adjustability of these two modes, allowing you to tweak the modes to your individual taste. These customization parameters are dimension, panorama, and width. These adjustments make it easier for you to tailor the sound for your individual equipment, room, and preference. The biggest advantage of Dolby Pro Logic II is that it creates new, dynamic surround sound for older media such as VCR tapes. It also serves as a big boost for normal television broadcasts, creating a more realistic surround sound.

Figure 2.7
If you are looking for a surround sound format for VHS tapes and standard definition cable broadcasts, Dolby Pro Logic II is a good choice

6.1 and 7.1 Channel Formats

Whereas the previously-mentioned surround sound formats use five speakers, there are new formats that use six and seven speakers (see Figure 2.8). THX EX is a joint venture between LucasFilm THX and Dolby Digital. This format is known as Dolby Digital EX. THX Surround EX is a new 6.1 format that uses five speakers just like Dolby Digital, but it also includes a matrixed rear center channel. Just as you have a left, right, and center channel in the front of your home theater, THX EX uses a right rear, left rear, and rear center channel. The use of a rear center channel provides more seamless transitions when a sound moves from one side of the rear speakers to the other. Today, very few DVDs are encoded with this format, but these emerging formats are gaining support. If your budget allows, buying a receiver with THX EX surround decoding provides even more realistic sound, but most budget home theater users will choose to go with 5.1 channel surround sound. THX EX surround receivers are also backward compatible, meaning they also play standard 5.1 Dolby Digital material.

Figure 2.8
Six and seven channel surround systems are becoming more common in high-end applications

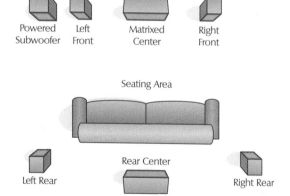

Another surround format, DTS ES, goes one step further than THX EX by incorporating a rear center channel that is discrete, not matrixed (as in THX EX). As with THX EX, this is a fairly new format, and few DVDs actually use it. The new formats that use rear center channels will slowly trickle into the budget home theater system, but at this point, they exist mainly in high-end systems. The rear center channels can offer some improvement in sound, but at this point there are only a select number of titles that take advantage of this technology. The rear center channel surround formats are a "nice to have" feature, but are certainly not required. Table 2.1 gives a thumbnail comparison between the various sound formats discussed in this chapter.

Table 2.1
Surround Sound Format Table

Surround Sound Format	Number of Channels	Media Type	Notes
Dolby Pro Logic	4	Television & VHS tapes	2 discrete, full-range audio channels, 1 matrixed front center channel, and 1 limited bandwidth low frequency effects channel
Dolby Pro Logic II	5.1	Television & VHS tapes	2 discrete, full-range audio channels, 3 matrixed full range (center, left rear, and right rear) channels, and 1 limited bandwidth rear channel
Dolby Digital	5.1	DVD, some satellite broadcasts, HDTV	Up to 5 discrete, full-range audio channels and a limited bandwidth low frequency effects channel
DTS	5.1	DVD	5 discrete, full-range audio channels and a limited bandwidth low frequency effects channel, lower compression than Dolby Digital
Dolby Digital EX, THX EX	6.1	Some DVDs	5 discrete, full-range audio channels, 1 full range rear center matrixed surround channel, and a limited bandwidth low frequency effects channel
DTS ES	6.1	Some DVDs	6 discrete, full-range audio channels and a limited bandwidth low frequency effects channel

So, with all the available choices for surround sound formats, you may be wondering which formats are essential and which are optional. Without question, Dolby Digital is essential. This format is included on virtually every DVD disc and is the sound format chosen for high-definition television. DTS and Dolby Pro Logic II are also important to look for when buying equipment. DTS is considered to be a better quality format than Dolby Digital, so when available, you will want to take advantage of the DTS format. The good news is that almost all home theater equipment available today has support for these three formats.

Dolby Digital EX and DTS ES are formats for the future. Although they currently don't have the mainstream acceptance of the standard 5.1 format of Dolby Digital, more and more DVD discs and home theater equipment are beginning to support these two formats. If you can find equipment that supports these formats, that's great; however, at this time, they can't be considered essential formats.

Audio Formats

Home theater systems are not used solely for watching DVD movies. Many people are finding value in the audio playback capabilities of surround systems. A high-quality surround system can re-create concerts and audio recordings with incredibly lifelike realism. Boasting much higher quality than a compact disc, these new audio formats look to revolutionize music listening. One note of warning: These new audio formats have yet to gain mainstream acceptance, and thus, the technology and hardware may change quickly.

New compression methods are also being used in these audio discs. Lossless compression ensures the highest quality recording and playback. Lossless compression is a compression scheme that does not alter the decoded signal at all. This requires the compression method to be more efficient at packing the data into the given area. Dolby Digital and DTS are both examples of "lossy" compression methods, meaning that information is discarded that cannot be uncovered even when uncompressed. These two compression schemes discard information to allow the data to fit into a smaller place. Unlike lossy compression methods, lossless compression methods can re-create the exact source when decompressed.

CD Audio

CD Audio has become the standard audio media format. Consumers know that the quality of a cassette tape's sound reproduction suffers the more times you play the tape. CD Audio, however, can be played again and again with no loss in sound quality. CD Audio uses a form of lossless compression and a sampling rate of 44.1 kHz. Sampling rate is the number of times per second that the original sound wave is measured, or "sampled", in order to be digitally reproduced. The higher the sampling rate, the more accurately the original sound can be reproduced. Since CD Audio uses a sampling rate of 44.1 kHz, that means it is sampling 44,100 points on the sound wave in a single second!

CD Audio uses two channels of audio (stereo) for playback. If you want to use all five speakers in your home theater system when listening to an audio CD, you'll have to use a surround format or digital signal processing (DSP) field that transforms two-channel audio into five channels of sound. Dolby Pro Logic II is an example of a surround sound format that will output sound from all five speakers when listening to a two-channel audio source.

DVD-Audio Soundtracks

DVD-Audio (or DVD-A) is a new format for high quality music recordings delivering much better quality than a typical compact disc can provide. A compact disc uses a sampling rate of 44.1 kHz, whereas DVD-Audio uses a much higher 192 kHz sampling rate. Due to the larger storage ability of the DVD media format, a DVD-Audio disc can contain as much as seven times the information a compact disc can store. This improved storage space allows DVD-Audio discs to contain much higher quality recordings and provide extra features much like those included with DVD movies. Much like a 5.1 channel DVD soundtrack for a movie, DVD-Audio discs can contain up to six channels of discrete audio. A special DVD player with DVD-Audio capabilities is required to listen to DVD-Audio discs. Look for the DVD-Audio designation if this sound format is of interest to you.

Super Audio Compact Disc

A competitor to DVD-Audio, Super Audio Compact Discs (SACDs) digitally encode compact discs with enhanced resolution. A SACD sounds much closer to the original recording than a typical CD. SACDs can hold up to six times the data of a normal compact disc, but they are more flexible than the DVD-Audio discs. One of the major advantages for the SACD format is that it provides normal, two-channel encoding that works in all existing compact disc players. However, to take advantage of the multichannel sound encoding of the SACD format, you need a new player capable of playing back SACD tracks. SACD uses a very high sampling rate of 2.8 MHz to produce improved clarity and realism in audio playback.

Both the DVD-Audio and SACD formats are gaining in popularity and availability, but these formats have barely started to penetrate the market. Although it is easy to find home theater equipment to play either format, it is often a tougher task to find media that uses these formats. Although it is still too early to declare a winner between the two, DVD-Audio is my bet to eventually win out. Many standard DVD players are being built with DVD-Audio playback capability. This will help the DVD-Audio format gain overall market acceptance.

Table 2.2 offers a comparison between a variety of audio formats.

Table 2.2
Audio Formats

PARAMETER	SACD	DVD-A	CD
Coding Method	DSD	PCM	PCM
Compression ratio	2:1	2:1	None
Frequency Response	0 Hz–100 kHz	0 Hz–48 Hz (six channel), 0 Hz–96 kHz (stereo)	5 Hz–20 kHz
Sampling Frequency	2.822 MHz	Up to 192 kHz	44.1 kHz
Dynamic Range	120 db	141 db	93db
Channels	Up to six	Up to six	Two

What is THX?

THX is a common—and commonly confused—buzzword in home theater. THX is an audio and video certification process for home theater products and theaters that meet a certain standard of quality. This certification is meant to ease home theater buying by identifying products that meet or exceed the high standards set by Lucasfilm's THX department. THX is often confused with Dolby Digital or DTS formats. Often people pose the question, "Do I need THX?" The answer, quite simply, is "No." If your budget affords the luxury of buying THX-certified components, you can be assured you are buying quality products, but they are not necessary for the budget consumer.

There are two different classifications: THX Select and THX Ultra. THX Ultra products (see Figure 2.9) meet or exceed very high performance criteria. THX Ultra products usually reside in high-end home theater components. Home theater receivers featuring THX Ultra certification can cost several thousand dollars. THX Ultra is a certification for theaters that will be larger than 3,000 cubic feet. THX Select, on the other hand, is recommended for smaller theaters, ranging in size up to 3,000 cubic feet.

Figure 2.9
Many high-end receivers, like this Onkyo TX-DS989, feature THX Ultra certification

CHAPTER 2

You may also see DVD discs marked "THX Digitally Remastered." Movies are created in mixing studios that are significantly larger than a typical home theater. Your home theater room is not even close to the size of the room for which the original soundtrack was prepared.

THX realized this problem and began to correct these tonal imbalances before the movies were released for the home consumer. Some of the steps THX takes in this process are reequalization, timbre matching, and bass management. The point of all these steps is to maximize home theater performance.

So, should you pay the high prices commanded by THX-certified components? If your budget allows, THX certifications certainly assure you that you are buying quality components. However, there are many very capable, quality home theater components that do not have the THX branding. You may be better off saving the added cost of THX-certified components and using your money in other ways. THX certification is in no way a required feature of a home theater system, especially in budget systems.

The Choice is Yours

You're now familiar with the common formats of surround sound. With the wide array of choices, you may be wondering which surround sound format to choose. Most budget systems won't consist of home theater receivers with Dolby Digital EX or DTS ES surround formats. For most budget home theater systems, most often you will want to select Dolby Digital for DVD playback. If DTS is available on the DVD, it is usually a preferred format due to its lower compression ratio. If you are watching normal broadcast television, Dolby Pro Logic II is probably your best option.

Most home theaters are used for many different purposes, including watching sporting events, television shows, and playing video games. Understanding the different formats and what types of media provide those formats allows you to maximize your home theater enjoyment. With this in mind, don't expect to get Dolby Digital from your old VCR tapes, but also make sure that when viewing a DVD, you select a digital format to experience the best audio reproduction possible.

3

Home Theater Audio Components

Now that you are familiar with the various surround sound formats, we delve into the necessary audio equipment to take advantage of these formats. Although your budget will be the driving factor in how much you spend, the process of finding the right receiver will be the same regardless of price. In this chapter, we also evaluate the seemingly attractive "home theater in a box" solutions. Of course, no audio component chapter is complete without a thorough and in-depth look at speakers.

Home Theater Receivers

The centerpiece of your home theater system is your home theater receiver. This piece of equipment is not only a big factor in how your system sounds and performs, but the receiver also serves as the traffic cop in the busy intersection of various signals. In most budget systems, the receiver processes the surround format, amplifies the signal, and decides which signal should be output to the TV monitor. It's easy to see why the receiver is considered the most crucial part in the home theater system.

The receiver's first purpose is to decipher the various sound formats you encounter when viewing different sources. For instance, for most DVDs, the receiver decodes either a Dolby Digital or DTS digital bit stream that ultimately outputs 5.1 channels of sound. For normal TV viewing, the receiver most likely receives a Dolby Pro Logic or stereo signal. Thankfully, most new receivers detect the correct format for you. Most receivers also let you select a different sound format manually if you so choose. However, because a stereo signal doesn't include the proper encoding, you cannot make the receiver play back in Dolby Digital. If you want to obtain surround sound from a stereo source, you need to select a surround sound format that creates matrix channels from a stereo source. Dolby Pro Logic II has this ability, but Dolby Digital does not. Most receivers do not give you the option of selecting the Dolby Digital format when the receiver detects that the input source is an analog signal.

How Powerful is Your Receiver?

Although the receiver is the brain of the operation, it also flexes it muscle as the brawn by providing amplification to the signal to allow for realistic volume levels. Most budget home theater receivers today consist of five channels of amplification, but, as we learned in the previous chapter, some systems—for today's newer surround formats—may consist of six or seven such channels. Most receivers are rated in watts, with an indication of how many channels of power the receiver has. For instance, a receiver rated at 100 watts per channel and consisting of five channels of amplification has a rating of 100 watts × 5.

Amplifier ratings in budget receivers can be confusing and misleading. Many times, different manufacturers rate their receiver's power at different resistance levels and only at a certain point of the audio frequency range. This skews the ratings, and makes the receiver's power numbers look better than they actually are.

When comparing receivers, you must be sure to compare them on a level playing field. Manufacturers frequently manipulate the facts of power outputs by claiming their receivers have "low resistance" (ohms). This tactic, of course, makes a receiver's power statistics look more appealing than they actually are. Some manufacturers, for instance, only rate at a certain frequency in the range, for instance 1,000 Hz. This allows them to find the frequency at which their amplifiers are most powerful and quote that power rating. A more meaningful power measurement is to look at the minimum amount of power supplied across the range of the entire audible frequency spectrum (20 Hz–20,000 Hz). Such a rating is more meaningful because television, music, and DVD movies feature sounds from the entire spectrum. A power rating that spans the entire spectrum gives you a much better idea of what the real power output of your home theater receiver will be.

To demonstrate, let's look at the three receivers in Table 3.1. Receiver X and Y both have claimed power of 100 watts. However, X is only rated at 1,000 Hz, whereas Y is rated across the entire range, giving Y's rating much more meaning. Also, notice the distortion of Receiver X at this power rating, seven times greater than the distortion in Receiver Y.

Table 3.1
Receiver Power Ratings Can Be Misleading

Receiver	Watts	Total Harmonic Distortion (THD)
X	100 watts @ 1,000 Hz into 6 ohms	.7
Y	100 watts into 6 ohms (20 Hz–20,000 kHz)	.1
Z	60 watts into 8 ohms (20 Hz–20,000 kHz)	.07

Now, let's dive deeper into this comparison. At first glance, you might think Receiver Y has more power than Receiver Z, but this is not necessarily true. Notice, again, how Receiver Y is rated into a lower resistance rating, thus raising its power rating. Most home theater speakers have 8-ohm resistance ratings. Therefore, you should strive to find receiver power ratings rated at 8 ohms, making their ratings more meaningful. Also, again notice that the distortion of Receiver Z is considerably less than the distortion quoted for Receiver Y. Given my choice of these three receivers, I would take the solid, clean power of Receiver Z.

So, should you rush out and buy 6-ohm speakers instead of 8-ohm speakers so your receiver will generate more power? Not necessarily. Although most home theater speakers have an 8-ohm resistance rating, some have lower resistance ratings. The lower resistance rating doesn't mean these speakers are better, it just means they offer more resistance and force your amplifiers to work harder to power them. This also means that your amplifiers will likely be able to output higher volume levels. For typical home theater usage, try not to purchase speakers that have a resistance rating lower than 6-ohm. Speakers featuring a lower resistance rating may lead your amplifier to overheating due to the increased workload of powering the speakers.

Features and Inputs

Because the receiver is going to be the centerpiece of your home theater, you want to make sure you are getting all the features that will allow you to enjoy and expand your home theater for years to come. An increasingly important feature of a home theater receiver is the number of digital inputs. Digital inputs are essential in home theater usage, as they are the type of connection necessary to use the digital surround sound formats, such as Dolby Digital and DTS. Digital inputs come in two forms: digital coaxial and optical inputs. See Figure 3.1.

Figure 3.1
Digital coaxial and optical inputs on a home theater receiver

Both inputs transport digital bit streams from an external device, such as a DVD player, to the receiver for decoding. The digital format results in unprecedented sound that is higher quality than sound from analog connections. DVD players, some digital cable boxes, satellite receivers, and video game consoles can often use a receiver's digital inputs. Currently, four digital inputs should be the minimum when shopping for a receiver. Also, ensure that the receiver has at least one of each type, coaxial and optical. This provides insurance in the event you purchase a device that has only one digital output format. Some audiophiles (aficionados of high-end audio) claim that they can hear differences between the two formats, but most budget home theater listeners are hard-pressed to find audible differences.

Your receiver not only handles digital formats, it also deals with analog signals such as the one from your VCR (see Figure 3.2). If you've ever hooked up a VCR, camcorder, or video game console to your TV, you're most likely familiar with analog connections. Often called RCA connectors, these yellow, red, and white wires transmit a video signal (yellow cable) and a stereo audio signal (red and white cables).

CHAPTER 3

Figure 3.2
A home theater
receiver, such as the
Onkyo TX-DS595
shown here, features
many inputs for
connecting other
devices

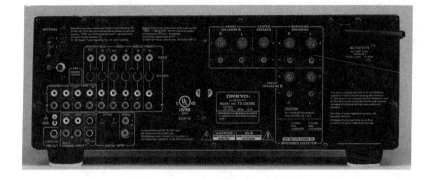

An essential feature on a home theater receiver is the ability to decode digital surround formats. Look for Dolby Digital and DTS decoding in a home theater receiver. Both are digital 5.1 channel surround formats. Dolby Digital is by far the most common, but more movies offering DTS decoding are emerging every day.

Dolby Pro Logic is a standard analog surround format that is featured on nearly every home theater receiver. An updated version, DPL II, is featured on many of the newer budget home theater receivers. If you plan on using your home theater for watching satellite television and sporting events, this feature will be important to you. If you will mainly be watching DVD movies that have a better digital surround format, this feature can be overlooked.

Receivers also offer a variety of speaker connections. Binding posts are the most common, and offer a much-improved connection over spring-loaded clips, as seen in Figure 3.3. Binding posts ensure that good connections are made between the receiver and the speaker wire, which translates into better sound with less interference.

Figure 3.3
Binding posts are
preferable to spring-
loaded clips; an
example of both can be
seen on the Onkyo TX-
L5 receiver

Home Theater Speakers

Your home theater's characteristics are most affected by the speakers you use. Most home theaters consist of five satellite speakers and a powered subwoofer. This configuration is commonly referred to as 5.1 channel surround sound. This setup is used by Dolby Digital, DTS, and Dolby Pro Logic signals to re-create soundtracks in your home theater.

The five speakers of a 5.1 channel setup physically surround the listening area. In the front, you will see a left speaker, a center channel, and a right speaker. Behind or to the sides of the listening area will be two surround speakers, on the left and the right. The powered subwoofer is typically concealed from site in a corner or to the side of the listening area. Each home theater room is unique, and compromises must be made based on space and appearance. For instance, some rooms may not have a rear wall on both sides of the listening area. A situation like this mandates using either a single wall-mounted speaker and a speaker on a stand, or two speakers on stands. Although it is optimal to have a rear or side wall to mount the rear speakers, you can still achieve great sound by using other placement options.

Shopping for speakers is a very subjective experience. Each person has different hearing and preferences, therefore different people prefer different speakers. However, there are characteristics to look for and certain quality-related specifications of speakers that can be scientifically measured and compared.

Matching Your Speakers

The most important thing when buying speakers is to ensure that they are voice matched. Voice matching (also called "timbre matching") means that the left, center, and right speakers all exhibit the same tonal characteristics. This becomes important due to the panning effects that are commonly used in movies. For example, perhaps there is a scene that shows a Ferrari moving from the left to the center to the right side of the television. If your speakers are not properly voice-matched, the Ferrari may sound like a Ferrari while it is on the left side, then may sound like a Ford Taurus when it moves into the center. Voice matching makes sure that the car sounds the same no matter where it is on the screen.

To ensure that your speakers are properly voice matched, buy speakers designed to be used together. Most manufacturers sell center channel speakers designed for use in conjunction with specific left and right channel speakers (see Figure 3.4). Using five identical speakers for your five satellite speakers assures proper timbre matching. Buying speakers that are voice matched allows for seamless transitions as the action moves around your home theater system.

Figure 3.4
The center channel speaker is used to reproduce dialogue and other sounds occurring in the center of the scene; shown here is an Atlantic Technology center channel from the T70 surround system

Although matching the front three speakers is considered essential, matching the rear speakers to the front speakers is less important. Although left-to-center-to-right panning effects are common movie elements, there are fewer front-to-rear panning effects. If possible, try to use speakers that match your front speakers, but it isn't as critical as matching your front trio of speakers.

Speaker Types

When you begin shopping for speakers, you'll encounter many different types—floor standing, bookshelf, dipole, bipole, and in-wall speakers are all common kinds of home theater speakers. We examine each type of speaker to ensure you pick the right ones for your home theater.

Floor-Standing Speakers

Floor-standing speakers are the largest of the speaker types, and they are often the most expensive. Floor-standing speakers, also called tower speakers, frequently consist of several woofers and tweeters.

WOOFERS AND TWEETERS

The term woofer refers to the particular driver of a speaker that typically produces sounds in the lower frequency range. A woofer usually features a larger cone than a tweeter.

The term tweeter refers to the normally small drivers of a speaker that reproduces high frequencies, such as 2000 Hz and above.

Figure 3.5
A floor-standing speaker is the largest of the speaker types, seen here is a Canton Ergo RC-A

Floor-standing speakers (see Figure 3.5) are generally the best for reproducing low-frequency sounds, especially those lower than 80 Hz. Because they are larger and taller, floor-standing speakers do not require the additional purchase of stands to elevate the speakers to ear level. Some floor-standing speakers even include powered subwoofers inside of them, making the use of an external powered subwoofer optional.

Bookshelf Speakers

Bookshelf speakers, as shown in Figure 3.6, are the most common speaker type for a budget home theater. Offering a good combination of size, performance, and cost, bookshelf speakers are often used for all five speakers in a 5.1 channel system. Bookshelf speakers need to be used in conjunction with a speaker stand or, as their name implies, placed on a shelf to raise them to ear level.

Figure 3.6
Bookshelf speakers,
such as the Aperion
Audio 512D, offer
good performance
and great value

Bookshelf speakers usually feature two drivers, a single woofer, and a tweeter. They need to be teamed with a powered subwoofer for home theater usage. Bookshelf speakers can save space and provide great sound. The speakers can be used as front, center, or rear speakers with great results.

Dipolar and Bipolar Speakers

Dipolar and bipolar speakers are variations on a typical speaker. These speaker types consist of an enclosure with multiple driver sets facing different directions. As its name implies, bipolar speakers consist of two speakers operating in phase with each other. A dipolar speaker configuration consists of four speakers, again with two sets of drivers firing towards the front and two firing to the rear with the front and rear speakers operating out of phase from each other.

PHASE

Speakers move forward and backward, making waves of air that create sound. When two speakers are working "out of phase" from each other, one speaker pushes outward while the other pulls inward. The first speaker's sound wave is at a peak while the second speaker's sound wave is at a low point.

Dipolar speakers (see Figure 3.7) tend to create an empty area directly to the side of the speaker, relying on sound waves reflecting off walls and ceilings to create a wider, more spacious surround field. Dipolar speakers are typically used by people who want to feel encompassed by the sound. However, dipolar speakers are not as good at re-creating a direct sound as a bipolar or direct radiating speaker.

Dipolar and bipolar speakers are typically used for surround speakers, as they can create a more enveloping sound field. Due to their design, bipolar speakers can be wall mounted. When your listening area is up against a wall or space is limited, bipolar or dipolar speakers may be a good option for you. Placement of the rear speakers will differ between bipolar and dipolar and with each individual room. It is usually best to decide what type of speaker enclosure you prefer, then examine your room to see if that type of speaker will work in your room. We explore speaker placement in more detail in the later chapters.

CHAPTER 3

Figure 3.7
The Atlantic
Technology IWTS
20SR is an eample
of a dipolar surround
sound speaker

In-Wall Speakers

In-wall speakers offer a more permanent, but less intrusive surround sound solution, as shown in Figure 3.8. In-wall speakers are placed into the wall, so that the front of the speaker is nearly flush with the wall. Often, the protective grill is painted to match the color of the wall. Although they save space, in-wall speakers generally do not perform as well as free-standing speakers, because of the space-saving compromises that must be made. Also, in-wall speakers use the wall as their enclosure, which puts them at a disadvantage over speakers using a designed enclosure.

Figure 3.8
In-wall speakers, such
as the Atlantic
Technology IWTS 20SR,
are unintrusive

Speaker Features

The speaker's quality of sound is without a doubt up to individual interpretation, but *Home Theater Solutions* helps you identify what speaker features to look for when shopping. Bi-amping and bi-wiring are two features commonly found on more expensive home theater speakers. Crossover network, frequency response, and a speaker's efficiency are all characteristics that are easily compared between different speakers.

Bi-amping/Bi-wiring

Bi-wiring is a common practice for high-end applications and home theater users who want to ensure they are getting the absolute best performance possible from their speaker system. The term bi-wiring refers to running two separate sets of speaker cables from a power source, such as a home theater receiver to a speaker. The theory behind bi-wiring is that bass frequencies can overpower the rest of the signal, thus causing the overall sound to suffer. Fans of bi-wiring point to better sound reproduction in the higher frequencies with less distortion.

Speakers have two connection points for the power source, a positive and negative terminal. Speakers that feature the ability to be bi-wired have two sets of positive and negative terminals. One set is connected to the high-frequency driver and the other set is connected to the low-frequency driver. These speakers usually feature a "jumper" that connects the positive terminal from the low-frequency driver to the positive terminal on the high-frequency driver. Likewise, there is also a "jumper" that connects the negative terminals. These jumpers allow a speaker with bi-wire ability to be powered by a single set of wires, if you don't want to bi-wire the speakers.

To bi-wire your speakers, you need to remove the metal jumpers that connect the two sets of speaker terminals. You also need to connect two sets of speaker wires to your receiver or other power source. After this is done, connect one set of speaker cables to the low-frequency positive and negative terminals and the other set of speaker cables to the high-frequency positive and negative terminals.

The process of bi-amping goes even further by using two separate power sources to power the separate high- and low-frequency components of a speaker. Bi-amping also requires a speaker to have bi-wiring ability. The thought behind this process is again that the low, bass frequencies will overpower the rest of the signal and increase distortion. Bi-amping is a high-end practice that is not very common in a typical home theater solution.

Sensitivity Rating

An important feature to look for in a home theater speaker is a sensitivity rating. Sensitivity, or efficiency, is measured in decibels. Sensitivity is calculated by measuring how loudly a speaker plays when given one watt of power. The higher the number, the louder the speaker plays back when given a certain amount of watts. For example, a speaker with a sensitivity rating of 91 db reproduces 91 db of sound from a single watt of power under standardized settings.

Sensitivity rating is an important feature in speakers that will be featured in a budget home theater system. A speaker that features high sensitivity plays louder than a speaker with low sensitivity when given the same amount of power. This allows the power source to achieve an acceptable playback volume with less power. This helps to keep the amplifiers working easier and minimizing distortion that happens when an amplifier is pushed hard.

Frequency Response

Frequency response is the entire range of frequencies that a speaker can reproduce. A typical human can hear sounds as low as 20 Hz and as high as 20,000 kHz. Although no single speaker in your system will cover this entire range, it is important to ensure that your system as a whole covers the range. Floor-standing speakers typically have the best frequency response. Bookshelf speakers usually offer a very good frequency response, often going as low as 50 Hz and as high as 20,000 kHz. Keep in mind that your powered subwoofer will be used to re-create the low-frequency effects, typically below 80 Hz.

Flatness, Imaging, and Dispersion

Other things to look for when selecting speakers are a flat response, good imaging, and the dispersion of the signal. Flat response may sound negative, but it is actually a good characteristic to look for in a speaker. When a speaker exhibits a flat response, it can represent different frequencies throughout the range without getting louder or softer. Imaging is the ability to re-create the spatial feeling of a recording and envision the actual position of the sounds at the time of initial recording. Dispersion of the signal is how well a speaker spreads its sound across the listening area. Many speakers sound wonderful when they are directly in front of you, but try listening to them while off to the side of the speakers. The results may surprise you. This is referred to as off-axis sound and is very important if your seating area is spread over a large area.

To evaluate the flatness, imaging, and dispersion of a speaker, it is necessary to develop a frame of reference. The easiest way to do this is to find a movie scene or music selection you are familiar with. Listen to the selection on a particular set of speakers. Then listen to the same selection again, except on a different set of speakers. When doing this, try to keep as many conditions as possible consistent and only change the speakers, so you can evaluate the speaker's performance in a controlled environment.

As you listen, move around the listening area and try to evaluate the overall sound in different areas of the listening area. Stand directly to the side or even behind the speakers and listen to the sound. Does it still sound as good as it did when you were in front of the speakers? If so, these speakers possess good off-axis sound. Does the selection seem to be a wide, spacious sound that surrounds you? If so, these speakers offer a good dispersion pattern.

When you listen to the selection, close your eyes and listen to the selection. As you listen, can you imagine the positioning of the instruments and vocals? If so, the speakers feature good imaging. Sit in the center of the speakers and observe the imaging of the speakers. Now move to the right or left side of the speakers and see if the imaging suffers.

There are no definitive answers as to which speakers have the best characteristics. These traits are very subjective. The important thing is to establish what speakers sound best to your personal tastes. As you listen to the selection numerous times, it should become easier for you to identify the characteristics that suit your personal tastes more easily.

Connections

Lastly, make certain the speakers you are selecting have a good, solid connection type. Look for good quality, gold-plated binding posts on your speakers to assure quality connections. Binding posts are a type of connection on the speaker that connects the speaker wire coming from your receiver or amplifier to the speaker. Binding posts are sometimes referred to as "5-way" binding posts. This means they can accept bare wire, spade connectors, pins, and banana plugs. Banana plugs are a good way to assure good connections that minimize oxidation, which cause your sound to suffer.

Powered Subwoofers

A powered subwoofer can make all the difference in a home theater system. A subwoofer has a very limited job—to re-create sounds from a small segment of the frequency spectrum, usually in the 20 Hz to 120 Hz range. These are the frequencies where the deep, bass-heavy sounds hang out. The subwoofer is responsible for re-creating the earth-shaking steps of a dinosaur and the thunderous explosion from your favorite action movie. With their large speaker cones, a subwoofer moves much more air than bookshelf or floor-standing speakers, allowing you to feel the movie in addition to just hearing it.

Powered subwoofers are the .1 of a 5.1 surround system. The .1 designation symbolizes that the low frequency effects channel is a limited bandwidth channel. Subwoofers are attached to the dedicated low frequency effects channel, usually through a single cable from the receiver. Subwoofers vary in size and shape, ranging from a small 6.5-inch woofer all the way up to 12-inch woofers. Typically, the larger the speaker cone, the more earthshaking the subwoofer will be due to the large speaker's ability to move more air.

You may have noticed that to this point we've only mentioned powered subwoofers (see Figure 3.9). Powered refers to the fact that the subwoofer does not use the receiver's internal amplifiers to generate sound. A powered subwoofer is powered by a dedicated amplifier. Typical amplifiers range from 100 watts to over 500 watts of power. During movie playback, the large woofer needs a solid amplifier to be able to accurately re-create the deep, earthshaking tones with distortion. Subwoofers usually have many more features than a typical speaker. Subwoofers normally feature a variable crossover, phase control, and gain control.

> ▶ A variable crossover allows you to set the frequency at which the subwoofer begins to pick up a signal. When the crossover frequency is set to 80 Hz, the subwoofer re-creates all signals 80 Hz and under.

> ▶ A phase control switch typically dictates if the woofer is "in phase" or "out of phase." This setting allows you to properly set your subwoofer to match the phase of your main speakers, regardless of positioning in the room.

> ▶ Gain control sets how much power is being produced by the amplifier. Gain control allows the powered subwoofer to match the output level of the other speakers in the system. If the subwoofer is not loud enough at a given volume, you can adjust the gain control to allow the subwoofer's amplifier to produce more sound.

CHAPTER 3

Figure 3.9
A powered subwoofer
helps re-create a
realistic experience

There are two types of enclosures for powered subwoofers: ported and sealed. A ported enclosure features at least one port hole that allows sound from inside the enclosure to escape. A sealed enclosure has no such holes. A sealed enclosure usually produces a more accurate sound, but does not produce volume levels as high as those achieved with a ported enclosure. Also, a sealed enclosure can help a subwoofer produce lower frequencies than a ported subwoofer. A ported subwoofer is usually more efficient, producing higher volume levels, but often at the expense of accuracy. Most budget subwoofers are ported, allowing them to produce more sound with less amplification.

Home Theater in a Box Solutions

The novice home theater buyer can be tempted by the idea of buying an entire system in one box. Commonly referred to as "HTBs," all-in-one solutions are attractive to the novice consumer due to their simplicity and ease of setup (see Figure 3.10). HTB solutions generally come with a DVD player, a receiver, five satellite speakers, and a subwoofer. These all-in-one solutions can usually be found at a competitive price, making them even more attractive.

However, with this added simplicity usually comes a great reduction in sound quality. Often, the HTB solutions do not allow much, if any, expandability or upgrades for the future. A common problem is that all the amplifiers in the system are housed inside the subwoofer. In addition, many use proprietary connection methods that keep you from using the speakers separate from the powered subwoofer or vice versa.

The biggest shortcoming of these solutions is their speakers. They are usually in plastic cabinets and feature cheap, paper-cone speakers, resulting in poor sound quality. Most subwoofers included with these packages leave much to be desired. Typically, the subwoofer component of these packages consist of a 6.5 inch woofer, which cannot move as much air as the larger powered subwoofers typically found in budget home theater systems (it therefore will not create the house-rattling force of a larger subwoofer).

Figure 3.10
An Onkyo HT-S493DV
home theater in a box
provides value, but
sacrifices quality

An all-in-one solution certainly has some benefits. Ease of shopping, setup, and price are all factors that make these solutions attractive to consumers. These solutions are also commonly found at many of the large electronics superstores. Despite their advantages, I feel in most cases consumers are better served by putting together their own home theater system—one that provides a much higher quality sound and a nice upgrade path for future components.

Separates

If you ask your local audio/visual expert to recommend a home theater system, he may point you in the direction of separates. Buying "separates" means buying a preamplifier processing component and an amplifier component. Home theater receivers combine these two elements into one component, simplifying the setup. Many audiophiles prefer the sound of a separate component system.

Separate systems offer advantages in sound quality, but also in future flexibility. (See Figure 3.11.) By separating the switching, decoding, and processing of the signal from the amplification of the signal, the overall quality is increased. Stand-alone amplifiers are better at producing large amounts of wattage without distortion. The amplifiers used for separate systems are typically of better quality than those that are used within home theater receivers.

Unfortunately, separate systems are often expensive, but by using a separate processor component and amplification component, you get extended upgrade ability. If a new surround sound format comes out, you could replace only the processor component. If the new format requires another amplifier, you can add another amplifier without having to replace all of your amplifiers. With this level of performance and future-proofing, however, comes a price tag. Separates are often found in high-end home theater systems, and these systems are usually much more expensive than a home theater receiver.

Figure 3.11
A high-end system consists of separate components, such as this Integra Research RDC-7 processor

You can get a high-quality home theater receiver that performs admirably, usually for less than the price of the processor component of a separate system. When building a home theater system on a budget, separates probably aren't the option you will want to pursue, unless you have a large budget.

Remote Controls

An often overlooked potential trouble spot is the remote control. Home theater systems can be large and cumbersome to control, but universal remote controls can greatly simplify the overall control of your home theater. Home theater systems consist of many components, all of which undoubtedly come with a remote control. To operate your entire system, you need to use buttons or commands from each of the remotes. This requires you to either use all the remotes or incorporate the necessary commands into a single remote that can control your entire theater.

Universal remote controls come in many shapes and sizes. You can pick up a $20 universal remote at your local electronics dealer, or you can go all out and purchase a $300 touch screen LCD remote control with unlimited expandability. (See Figure 3.12.) No universal remote you purchase will have every necessary command to run your system. You can use preprogrammed codes to get the remote to perform the desired function. Codes are built in by the remote manufacturer that tell the remote what infra-red signal to send when you press a desired button. However, your remote may not feature a preprogrammed code for all your devices, so learning ability is crucial in a universal remote. Learning ability allows a remote to "listen" to the code being sent from the original remote, learn the code, and save it, allowing you to send this code anytime in the future. Obviously, a cheaper universal remote is limited in learning ability and memory, but with a smaller budget system, it might work perfectly for you. What you should do, though, is make a list of all devices you need to control, and then research the universal remote to see if it possesses preprogrammed codes for your devices. If it doesn't have all the necessary preprogrammed codes, ensure that it has learning ability so it can learn the remote commands that it isn't able to re-create.

Figure 3.12
Home theater remotes
can be simple or
extensive, as seen here
in a comparison
between a Radio Shack
universal remote and an
Onkyo CHAD LCD
touch screen remote

Switching between television watching and viewing a DVD will most likely require the use of
many buttons that are likely on several remotes. For instance, you have to select the correct
input on your television, the correct input on your receiver, and then press Play on your DVD
player. Considering you will often be making this switch, a macro can save you lots of time and
frustration. A macro is a series of commonly repeated remote commands that are saved in a
sequence that can be recalled with a single press of a button. For instance, you may have a
macro to turn your television, home theater receiver, and DVD player on. To do so, you record
the TV power on command, home theater power on command, and DVD player power on
command into a single macro, enabling you to turn on all of your components with a single
button press. The ability for a remote to record macro commands is a feature you should look
for when buying a universal remote. Macro commands can greatly simplify common tasks such
as turning on your home theater system.

We've now explored all the different audio components in a typical home theater. When buying
a system, it helps to go into the shopping process with an idea of what type and size of
components you are looking to buy.

4

Home Theater Video Components

Chances are when you hear the term "home theater," the first image you picture is a wall-sized television screen. Well, you don't need a huge television to create a home theater. In fact, many budget home theater buyers often incorporate their existing television set, even sets as small as 27 inches. Of course, if you do decide you can't live without that 60-inch television, we give you some tips and hints for buying a suitable set, one that won't become obsolete tomorrow—despite today's changing standards.

Today, DVD players are becoming a standard in home theater (yes, even in budget systems). As we have discussed previously, DVD players provide a digital bitstream that is received by your home theater receiver. This digital signal is then translated into the surround sound that is output through the speakers. The DVD player also provides crystal clear video pictures, which, unlike analog VHS tapes, do not degrade with use.

Although a DVD player provides incredible digital sound and unblemished video signals, it can't replace your VCR. A DVD player, for instance, cannot record your favorite television shows. A device that can, however, is called a personal video recorder (PVR), which records your television shows onto a hard disk drive just like the one in your computer. A PVR is similar to a VCR because it records television programming, but it is far superior in the quality and flexibility of its recordings. By recording shows digitally onto the hard drive, a PVR can store and replay television shows and movies for instant access. PVRs also offer the added ability to time shift programming, enabling you to watch television shows on your own time.

If you are a movie fan, you've probably amassed a large collection of VCR tapes. Don't fret that you'll have to throw them all away because they're obsolete. With the introduction of Dolby Pro Logic II, VCR tapes have gotten a new life (see the "Video Cassette Recorders" section to find out how). This is good news, of course, because when you build your home theater system with some of your existing equipment, it allows you to increase your budget for new equipment.

In this chapter of *Home Theater Solutions*, we explore the different components that make up the gorgeous pictures that help immerse you in the experience.

Televisions and Projectors

The television will likely be the most expensive piece of equipment in your home theater system. And it should be. Televisions typically have a long life, making the selection important because it will be part of your home theater system for years. Televisions span a wide range of sizes and prices. A good 32-inch CRT tube-based television costs around $500, whereas a huge, rear projection, high-definition television goes for around $3,500. You will have to determine what you can afford.

Today, the majority of households have at least one CRT tube-based television, which is the most common and cost-effective solution for displaying video in your home. Standard CRT tube-based televisions range from small, inexpensive units to large televisions capable of displaying today's highest resolution formats.

If size is the most important factor, then rear projection television (RPTV) sets must be considered. These sets, often dubbed "big screens" by the average consumer, range in size from 40 inches to over 70 inches. RPTV sets use three different colored guns and a series of mirrors to project images onto their huge display screens. Although these sets typically cost more than most CRT tube-based television sets, they offer a larger screen format and better quality.

Front projection displays are the ultimate in size and quality. Unrivaled by CRT screens for size, many high-end dedicated home theater rooms rely on front projection to display the video signal. Although these incredible units are the biggest format available, they are also by far the most costly. These units typically cost several thousand dollars for the projector alone, and also require a high-quality screen to achieve optimal picture quality and an optimal viewing environment, such as a dark room..

Plasma television sets are just beginning to hit consumer markets. These ultra-thin, sleek sets feature a "cool factor" that gets everyone's attention. Plasma displays are currently available in the forty- to sixty-inch range, and offer very nice picture quality. Of course, with new technology comes a high price tag. Currently, plasma television sets cost two to three times more than a comparable rear projection television set while offering similar quality. The real draw of plasma television sets is the space saving cabinets that allow them to be hung on walls like a picture frame.

CRT Tube-Based Televisions

The most common type of television today, and probably the one you currently have in your home, is a tube-based television that relies on a cathode ray tube, commonly called CRT, to display images. (See Figure 4.1.) Here's how it works: A set of electron beams projects light onto a phosphor-coated screen that glows when struck by the beam. This series of events ultimately leads to the image you see on your television screen.

Figure 4.1
A CRT tube-based
television is the most
common type of
television today

Today, most CRT tube-based televisions use interlaced scan. Interlaced scan draws half of the lines on the television screen in one pass, then comes back and fills in the other half of the lines on the next pass. It repeats this refresh process between 50 and 60 times every second. For example, on the first pass, an interlaced scan television draws all the odd lines. It then repeats the process, but this time draws all the even lines. A typical television consists of about 520 horizontal lines, so each pass refreshes about 260 lines.

In Figure 4.2, you can see a re-creation of how an interlaced image is drawn onto the television screen. In the picture on the left, the illustration shows an image after the first pass, with half of the lines drawn on the screen. The picture on the right shows the image when the second pass is almost finished. The bottom picture shows what the finished image looks like.

Figure 4.2
Interlaced scan, the
most common display
method on CRT tube-
based televisions,
refreshes every other
line during each pass

First Pass

Second Pass

Final Image

Most CRT tube-based televisions have a curved glass front, but some of the newer ones, such as Sony's FD Trinitron Wega series, feature a completely flat glass front. If you've been to a local retailer, you've probably noticed these televisions. The flat picture screen creates a more film-like picture than the curved glass front screen, especially in the corners of the screen. Another advantage of the flat picture screen is that it allows a clear view from an increased variety of viewing angles. Curved screens also slightly distort the image. You may have noticed this when looking at horizontal lines on your television; often they appear curved instead of completely straight.

CRT tube-based televisions have many advantages over comparable RPTV sets. CRT tube-based televisions require little or no maintenance after the initial setup is performed. Because CRT tube-based televisions are the most common on the market today, they are also the least expensive. CRT tube-based televisions also have good dependability, last for years, and come in many sizes (so you can easily find exactly what you are looking for). And because with CRT televisions you are seeing the original image instead of a projected image, they can provide a brighter, more optically correct image.

Like all types of televisions, though, CRT tube-based televisions also suffer some drawbacks. Due to the nature of the glass and electronics inside, CRT tube-based televisions are heavy compared to other television types. Also, CRT tube-based televisions are only available in sizes up to 40 inches. Keep in mind that due to their relatively new technology, the flat screen tube televisions are considerably more expensive than their curved-screen counterparts. Finally, don't forget that you'll most likely need to place a CRT tube-based television on top of a stand or in an entertainment center to raise it to eye level when seated. If you don't currently own a stand or an entertainment center, remember to consider them and their costs when shopping.

Rear Projection Television Sets

Picture your ultimate home theater. See a huge television nestled right in the middle? You've probably just pictured a rear projection television (RPTV) set. If you are looking to add a television larger than 40 inches to your home theater, an RPTV is the type of television most likely to suit you, as RPTVs range in size from 40 inches to an incredible 70 inches, as shown in Figure 4.3. RPTVs can also offer amazingly crisp images.

Although RPTV sets have the potential to deliver jaw-dropping pictures with incredible detail, they often require a considerable amount of setup and calibration before they look their best. Unfortunately, an RPTV set that hasn't been properly calibrated does not look acceptable. When you purchase an RPTV set, it will likely arrive with a less than optimal picture that requires its lenses to be focused and electronics to be converged in order to get ultimate performance. But after it's properly tweaked, an RPTV set offers a stellar image that's hard to beat.

The ultimate but costliest way to get an RPTV properly tweaked is to have a technician from the Imaging Science Foundation (ISF) come to your home and set up your RPTV. The ISF specializes in bringing out the best in rear projection television. Many rear projection owners hire ISF-certified technicians to perform a series of calibrations to their televisions. Depending on the type and number of calibrations the technician performs, the cost of these sessions ranges from $300 to over $500.

To get the best picture, ISF technicians use sophisticated color analyzing tools and advanced techniques. Most television sets come from the factory with "red push." "Red push" is a term commonly used by technicians to describe a television that displays too much red color according to NTSC color standards. ISF Technicians will typically calibrate your set to 6500 degree Kelvin white. They will also ensure that the television is producing this accurate white (not too much red or blue) over the entire brightness spectrum. Accurate color rendition is important because it if not set correctly, whites can look dingy or blue, and blacks may look green. Luckily, many sets today come from the factory with a "Pro" or "Theater" mode that is typically calibrated very close to NTSC standards. ISF technicians often perform difficult focusing maneuvers inside the television and use special service technician menus that allow increased control over your television settings.

Even if you aren't ready to throw down $500 to get a professional calibration, you can still perform many of these techniques yourself. Also, many of the ISF technicians are prominent members of Internet message boards. If you have Internet access, you can read and correspond with some of the top ISF calibration professionals across the United States. Many times, these technicians offer helpful advice about which brands and models of television sets create the best picture, both pre-calibration and after a full calibration.

If you want to learn more about the ISF, check out their Web site at www.imagingscience.com.

RPTV sets are the most common display types in home theater systems. While RPTVs often use a CRT similar to the one in a CRT-based television to produce the picture, how it displays it is very different. RPTV sets form a small image of what is to be shown on the screen on three independent CRTs, an LCD screen or a DLP, then through a series of lenses, that image is focused onto a large mirror that reflects the image onto a projection panel that then casts the image onto the screen. One advantage of this technology is that the screen that the image is projected onto is flat. This flat surface gives you the same advantages of the flat display CRT tube-based televisions.

Figure 4.3
Rear projection television (RPTV) sets range in size from 40 inches up to 70 inches

Because they are much larger than CRT tube-based televisions, RPTV sets usually have higher price tags. You can expect to pay between two and five thousand dollars for a high-quality rear projection television set. Most RPTVs come with an enclosure that brings the viewing screen up to eye level without an additional stand. Although RPTV sets can be much larger in size than CRT tube-based televisions, they often don't weigh much more. Most RPTV sets feature rollers on the bottom, so you can easily move the television by yourself.

RPTV sets offer large screens for decent prices, but they require more effort to obtain a great picture. You should always go to your local retailer and compare each brand and model to find which model looks best to you. Toshiba, Mitsubishi, Sony, and Pioneer are examples of manufacturers that make high-quality RPTV sets. Pioneer Elite sets are usually considered the best RPTV sets, but they also carry a higher price tag. Most television sets, including RPTVs, arrive with very high brightness and contrast levels. This is often referred to as "torch mode." Manufacturers want their television to stand out on the showroom floor, and having a very bright picture often grabs a potential buyer's attention. When comparing television sets, ensure that the settings are similar on all the sets you are comparing.

Front Projection Displays

Front projection displays are the display type most commonly found in high-end systems. Front projection systems consist of a projector, often found on one side of the room, and a screen that the image is projected onto on the opposite side of the room. Front projection displays use technology similar to RPTVs, taking a small image and using a series of lenses to project the image onto the screen. You're probably familiar with a front projection system; movie theaters use a front projection system.

Front projection systems offer the advantage of having almost unlimited size potential. Front projection systems also offer incredible pictures, showing amazing detail for such a large display. Typically, front projection sets can display very high-resolution formats that most RPTVs aren't capable of displaying.

As awesome as front projection displays are, though, there are also many negatives associated with them. Obviously, cost is a big drawback. An entry-level projector likely costs at least $2,000. A separate display screen is also required to obtain a worthy image. Moreover, front projection systems are rated for brightness (measured in lumens), and if the projector doesn't have enough lumens for your room, the picture may not be bright enough—particularly if your room has many windows. Projectors use bulbs in their display, and the bulbs are not only costly but suffer from a short life span. A typical bulb lasts around 1,000 hours before it needs to be replaced.

Keep in mind that front projection systems are not meant for everyday use. Most projectors don't even have a television tuner included, so you need to use the projector in conjunction with a device that has a television tuner, such as a VCR. Most often, front projection systems are used for dedicated home theater rooms that have few windows or possess "black out" shades.

Plasma Displays

Plasma displays are the wave of the future. (See Figure 4.4.) Unlike CRT tube-based televisions and RPTV sets, plasma displays are extremely thin and light. You've probably seen the commercial with the big television hanging on the wall. The television monitor in that commercial is an example of a plasma display. Plasma displays use a series of small cells to create a picture. Each cell possesses three smaller elements, called pixels, that are red, green, or blue.

Plasma television monitors offer a high "wow" factor, but this comes with a very steep price tag. An entry-level plasma monitor, around 40 inches, can cost over $6,000. Plasma technology is still in its infancy, so advances in technology and manufacturing will continue to drive down the price and increase the quality. Current plasma displays can have problems with cell burnout, meaning that a cell quits producing color, leaving just a black spot on the screen. Also, some plasma screens have trouble displaying fast-action programming (such as sporting events).

Figure 4.4
Plasma displays, such as this Integra PLA-50V1, are very slim and light, but also very expensive

Obviously, the attraction of plasma screens is the incredibly small size of the television's cabinet. Plasma screens range in size from 40 inches to over 50 inches. If your space is very small and you are set on having a large display screen, a plasma display may be a solution. However, you might want to let the technology improve and prices drop before opting for a plasma display.

High Definition Television

High definition television (HDTV) is an emerging trend in broadcast video. HDTV is a form of digital television (DTV). While currently available in most large cities, HDTV is beginning to become available in smaller areas. HDTV produces an information-packed digital signal that results in increased picture quality. Not just an improvement in video quality, HDTV also features enhanced audio, utilizing the Dolby Digital surround sound format.

Typical non-HDTV broadcasts are analog standard definition signals consisting of 480 interlaced lines. Although there are several competing formats of HDTV signals, the most common format consists of 1,080 interlaced lines, referred to as 1080i. As you can see, HDTV formats can offer over twice the resolution of a standard signal, providing a sharper, more detailed image.

As mentioned, there are several different HDTV signal standards. The main competitor to the 1080i is a format consisting of 720 lines of resolution in a progressive scan format, called 720p. The "p" in 720p stands for progressive scan. Interlace signals draw every other line in a single pass, then another pass draws the remaining lines. Progressive scan works like a computer monitor by drawing each line on the screen in a single pass. Progressive scan starts with drawing the first line on the screen, followed by the second and third and so on. Each line is drawn in succession, which results in a smoother picture.

Another difference between standard definition and HDTV signals is the aspect ratio in which the picture is displayed. Standard definition signals use an aspect ratio of 4:3. This means the width of the display screen is 1.33 (four divided by three) times greater than the height. HDTV uses a wider aspect ratio of 16:9. This wider aspect ratio is often called widescreen or theater wide. (See Figure 4.5.) In a widescreen format, the width of the screen is 1.78 times as large as the height. A standard aspect ratio television appears almost square, whereas a widescreen television looks quite rectangular.

Figure 4.5
HDTV sets have a wide aspect ratio, which looks more like a movie theater's screen than a conventional television

High definition sounds great, right? However, as always, there are prices to pay before you can take advantage of an HDTV signal. Your current set is probably only capable of displaying a 480i signal. If you want to enjoy HDTV, you'll most likely have to purchase a new television set. When shopping for a new HDTV television, you'll encounter many options. Most HDTV sets are "HDTV ready" or "HDTV monitors." An HDTV-ready television set requires a special HDTV tuner that takes a digital signal and converts it into a signal recognizable by your television. Very few sets currently on the market feature an internal tuner capable of receiving an HDTV broadcast. A typical HDTV tuner costs around $600, in addition to the cost of the actual television set.

HDTV is growing closer to mainstream acceptance as more programming becomes available, but it will still take time before this new technology captures a large market. Most RPTV sets and nearly all plasma televisions possess the ability to display at least one of the two main high-definition standards of 1080i and 720p. Most RPTV sets are capable of displaying a 1080i signal, but few can display a 720p signal. The 720p format requires a very high scanning frequency. Most RPTV sets do not have the capability of operating at this scanning frequency, so they "up-convert" the 720p signal to a 1080i signal in order to display the image. Most high-definition tuners possess the ability to take a 720p signal and covert it into a 1080i signal, allowing your RPTV to display the picture.

Most large-market television studios have begun broadcasting a digital signal in tandem with the standard analog signal. Broadcasters will soon phase out the analog signal, broadcasting only the new digital signal. To continue using your old television sets, you'll soon need to buy a digital-to-analog converter that turns an incoming digital signal into an analog signal. You won't be able to take advantage of the increased high-definition signal quality with the converter, but you won't have to throw away your old television set either.

Currently, the majority of "HDTV-ready" monitors are RPTV sets. However, most of the RPTV sets only support the 1080i and 480p formats, and don't support the 720p format and the high-scanning frequency it requires. There are very few sets that can display a 720p format natively. There are some CRT tube-based televisions, such as the Sony Wega KV36HS500 and the Toshiba 36HF72, that are capable of displaying high-definition formats, but these sets are expensive compared to their rear projection counterparts.

HDTV standards continue to change as formats mature. One area of particular concern is the fact that almost every 2002 model and earlier HDTV-ready monitor has only component video input for accepting high definition signals. The latest standard for HDTV input is Digital Visual Interface (DVI). DVI is a digital connection between an HD tuner, commonly called a Set-Top Box (STB), and an HDTV-ready monitor.

The DVI input allows the HD signals to be encoded with content protection to keep people from reproducing high-definition signals. This copy protection has been dubbed HDCP, which stands for High-bandwidth Digital Copy Protection. HDCP allows digital content owners, such as television studios, to externally determine content-protection settings. The settings vary from allowing no reproduction, to allowing a limited number of reproductions, to allowing unlimited reproduction.

The DVI and HDCP inclusion have made many early-adopters of HDTV nervous. Their HDTV-ready monitors may become obsolete if some form of high-definition tuner is not created that will allow them to input a high-definition signal via component video inputs. As you can imagine, this does not sit well with the over 2.5 million people who currently own HDTV-ready monitors that do not have a DVI connection point.

DVD Players

Digital Versatile Disc (DVD) players are a "must have" in any home theater system. While gaining mainstream acceptance, DVD players have continued to advance in technology as their prices have continued to plunge. So what's the big deal? DVD players provide a much-improved picture over a conventional VCR. DVD players vary in price, from budget models for under $100 to high-end reference models costing several thousand dollars.

When shopping for a DVD player, you'll find hundreds of brands and models. All these players share the common feature of DVD playback, but many DVD players are packing in added features. Newer DVD players, for example, offer playback of other formats, such as SACD, DVD-Audio, MP3, and CDR playback.

DVD players link to your television set by one of the following types of connections:

- ▶ Composite
- ▶ S-Video
- ▶ Component

Composite Video

Composite video connections, shown in Figure 4.6, are very common inputs on a television. Although they are the most common connections, composite video connections offer the lowest grade of connection to your television. Red, green, and blue colors are all combined into a single 75-ohm resistance cable that connects from your source to your television. If you have S-Video or component inputs on your television set, you should try to use those. Chances are, you've probably got several composite cables lying around.

Figure 4.6
Composite video connections are very common, but the quality of connection is not as good as S-Video or component video connections

S-Video

S-Video is a newer display connection format that offers improved picture quality over composite cables due to separation of the video signal. S-Video separates the signal, producing a better picture with less conversion artifacts, which results in a cleaner picture that replicates the original source image more closely than when using composite video connections. S-Video connections are vastly superior to composite connections, and only slightly inferior to component connections. See Figure 4.7.

Figure 4.7
S-Video connections are fairly common and offer much improved signal quality over composite connections

Component Video

Component video connections, shown in Figure 4.8, are the newest connection form and also offer the best picture quality because component video connections split the signal into three individual cables. This splitting of the information allows better color separation and improves the picture quality. Most DVD players feature component video outputs; however, if your television doesn't have component video inputs, you cannot use this improved connection. Component cables use cable types similar to composite cables, and at first glance they may be mistaken for composite cables. High-quality composite cables can even be used as component cables, but you should ensure they are good quality and offer true 75-ohm resistance for optimal picture quality.

Figure 4.8
Component video connections are the preferred choice of connections between a DVD player and a television set

Component video connections offer some advantages not found in other connection methods (such as composite and S-Video). If your DVD player and television both offer progressive scan playback, for example, you can take advantage of this feature by using component video connections. Neither S-Video nor composite connections allow you to take advantage of the progressive scan format.

Besides having multiple video outputs, DVD players also have several types of audio connections. For digital surround formats, such as Dolby Digital and DTS, you need to use the digital audio output of your DVD player. Some DVD players feature an optical output, sometimes called a toslink connection. Other DVD players feature a digital coaxial connection, and some DVD players feature both types of digital connections. These digital connections allow the digital bitstream to be passed from the DVD player to the receiver, which then decodes this signal and re-creates the sound.

Some DVD players feature Dolby Digital and DTS decoding. The DVD players will decode the digital bit stream and send the signal to a home theater receiver that is Dolby Digital ready. A Dolby Digital ready receiver is a receiver that doesn't feature an onboard decoder to process a digital surround sound bit stream, but it does have six-channel analog inputs that allow it to receive a signal, amplify it, and produce Dolby Digital surround sound. This setup was very common in the late 90s, but has become rare today. If your home theater receiver features Dolby Digital and DTS decoding, there is no reason to buy a DVD player with decoding.

A new twist on the typical DVD player is the DVD-R. Much like a recordable compact disc or CD-R, a DVD-R is a DVD recorder. This device is capable of creating, often called "burning," a DVD. The appeal of these devices is the ability to record television, movies, photos, and even home movies onto a DVD that can then be transported anywhere. DVDs can store tremendous amounts of data allowing hours of full-motion video. However, there are many competing formats in the DVD-R arena, such as DVD-ROM, DVD-RAM, and DVD-RW, so steer clear of these devices until the standards settle.

Personal Video Recorders

A new entry to home theater systems is the personal television recorder (PVR). A PVR serves as a digital VCR that records and stores your programming on a hard disk, like your computer's disk drive. Two of the major brand names of PVR devices are Tivo and Replay. By using massive disk drives, these recorders can store over sixty hours of programming. (See Figure 4.9.)

Another selling feature of PVR devices is the "time shifting" ability of the recorder, something your old VCR absolutely cannot do. What is time shifting? Time shifting is the ability to delay the time you begin watching the program. For instance, you sit down to watch the big football game. About the time you settle in your recliner, the phone rings. If you answer the phone, you will miss the start of the game. If you start to record the game on your VCR, you won't be able to watch it until the game is completely over some three hours later. With a PVR device, you can pause live television. When you are finished with the phone call, simply unpause and begin watching where you left off. The game continues to record, but you watch it as it is recording. When you come to a commercial, simply skip ahead till the commercial break is over.

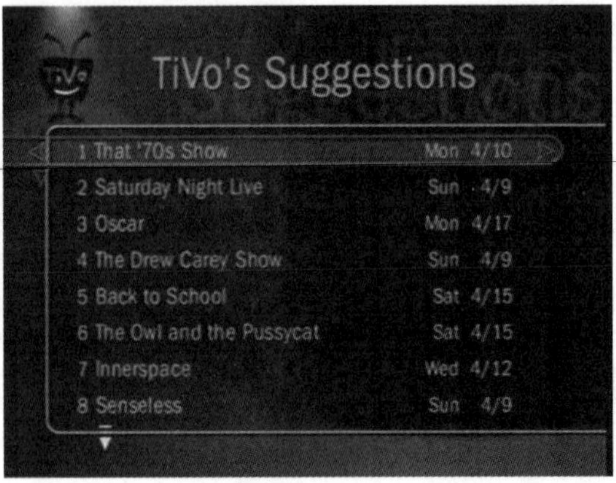

Figure 4.9
Personal video recorders (PVRs) offer advanced options for watching and recording television programming

As mentioned, because PVRs have huge storage capabilities, you can store many programs on the internal hard drive. This allows you to watch any program off the hard drive at any time, even while recording another show. The massive storage available lets you store digital copies of movies so you can watch them at any time as well. Some advanced PVR devices feature two tuners, allowing you to record one program and watch another program at the same time.

At night, PVR devices use your phone line connection or your home's Internet connection, if available, to download a seven-day program guide, as shown in Figure 4.10. This program guide is customized to your local area and programming options. You can browse the guide, and tell your PVR device which programs you want to record. These digital recorders also incorporate advanced capabilities that allow multiple recording options. For example, you can set the PVR device up to record each showing of your favorite show for the entire season. Some PVR recorders also allow you to select options to only record first showings, and not to record repeat showings.

Figure 4.10
PVR recorders offer seven-day program guides and advanced recording options

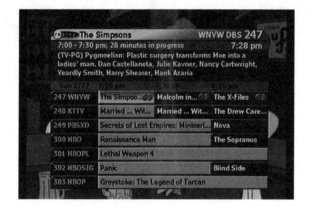

PVRs are sold in two different varieties: stand-alone and satellite-incorporated. Stand-alone recorders can be used to record local cable television programming, programming received from an antenna, or programming received via satellite dish. The PVRs that are incorporated with a satellite receiver offer integration for those consumers who subscribe to digital satellite services, such as Dish Network and DirecTV.

Stand-alone PVRs offer greater flexibility than those with satellites because they have a built-in cable/antenna tuner and the ability to connect to a satellite receiver, but if you subscribe to satellite programming, a stand-alone receiver does not allow you to change channels as quickly as an integrated satellite receiver/PVR unit does. This is because the infrared signals must be received from the PVR device and then conveyed to the satellite receiver. If you purchase an integrated PVR and a satellite receiver, you won't be able to record programming from local cable or over an antenna.

Video Cassette Recorders

When building a budget home theater system, integrating your existing equipment allows you to increase your budget in other areas of your system. Most consumers have a VCR lying around, and the VCR can still play a role in today's home theater system. A VCR gives you a simple, cost-effective way to store television programs and movies.

Over the years, you've probably accumulated a collection of your favorite movies on VHS tapes. You may not want to purchase the DVD version of a movie that you already own on VHS. If your receiver has Dolby Pro Logic II decoding, these VHS movies take on new life with the improved surround sound decoding.

A VCR can also be a great tool for archiving saved programs from a PVR. PVR devices have massive storage capability, but if you are running short on space, you can archive programming from your PVR device to a VHS tape for future playback.

Now that you are familiar with the audio and video components that make up a home theater, you can start to plan your budget to purchase these components.

5

Setting a Budget

If you've spent some time reading a typical home theater publication, you might be under the impression that a "typical" home theater costs well over $10,000. Although $10,000 systems definitely exist and probably do provide superior video and audio performance, most people don't have the luxury of dishing out $10,000 for their home theater. Having created and helped support a popular budget home theater website, www.cheaphometheater.com, I know that you can easily put together a great-sounding home theater system on a much smaller budget. In this chapter, we help you establish your own personal budget for your system.

Every home theater owner has different wants, needs, and available funds. You may prefer a huge television with a smaller speaker setup. Or, you may prefer a more robust speaker system with a smaller television monitor. Either way, setting a budget ensures that you can relax and enjoy your new system—instead of worrying about how you will pay for all the equipment.

In this chapter, we step through the budget-setting process. First, we establish a top dollar amount for your budget. Then, we identify components you currently own that can possibly play a role in your new system. After that, you'll need to recognize your preferences and decide if you are more interested in the video or the audio aspect of home theater. We finish by discussing some commonly overlooked factors that can push your system over its intended budget.

How Much Do You Have to Spend?

You have to determine how much you can afford to spend on a home theater system. Establish your maximum budget before you start shopping. For the purpose of this book, we set your total budget at $3,000 and use this budget throughout as we research, select, and assemble your hypothetical system. Most likely, your actual budget will not be exactly $3,000, but you can still use the techniques we discuss for your real budget.

An easy way to determine approximate spending on each component is to calculate the scale of your budget compared to our sample budget of $3,000. For example, if you only have $1,500 to spend, the scale calculates to .5 ($1,500/$3,000). Using this scale, if we spend $500 on a particular component, you can scale your purchase on that component to $250 ($500 × .5).

What Components Do You Already Own?

The easiest way to optimize your budget is to identify necessary components you already own. Most likely, you currently own at least one component of a home theater system that you could possibly incorporate into your new system. If you own a television, VCR, pair of speakers, or DVD player, all these components may be able to serve a purpose in your new system.

Your TV

When building a home theater system, the television is usually one of the biggest ticket items. If you are fortunate enough to already own a television suitable for a home theater, you should give serious thought to using your existing monitor. This frees up needed money in your budget for the rest of your components. If your existing television set is at least 32 inches (measured diagonally from top corner to bottom corner), you will likely not have to purchase a new set.

Although any television will do, most people won't be satisfied watching DVD movies on a 20-inch television monitor. With today's prices, a 32-inch set is a good starting point. If your television is smaller than this, you may want to plan on upgrading your set when building your new home theater.

Your VCR, DVD Player, or Laserdisc Player

As mentioned previously, a VCR can still play an integral role in a home theater system. If you currently have a VCR, specifically a stereo or "Hi-Fi" VCR, you should plan on using it in your new system. If you plan on buying a new VCR, make sure you buy a stereo VCR with four heads, which provides a better picture output than a VCR with only two heads. If you can use your current VCR, it may allow you to postpone purchasing a personal video recorder until the technology develops and becomes more widely accepted.

If you already have a functioning DVD player, you can most likely use your existing player in your new system. DVD players have improved over the years, but even the first DVD players made have the essential features, such as the ability to output digital sound, needed for a home theater system. If you plan on upgrading to a new video monitor capable of progressive scan playback, you should also consider purchasing a progressive scan DVD player. However, if you plan on using your existing television monitor and it isn't capable of progressive scan output, it is beneficial to use your existing DVD player.

Although DVD players are replacing laserdisc players, a laserdisc player can still serve a function in a home theater system. Laserdiscs have the ability to output Dolby Digital sound and good video quality, allowing you to enjoy a realistic theater experience. If you have a substantial collection of movies on laserdisc, you should incorporate your existing laserdisc player into your new system.

Your Speakers

If you currently own a speaker set, it too may be of use in your new system. The speakers can probably function well as left and right rear surround speakers. I don't recommend using an existing pair of speakers for the front left and right channels unless you have or can find a center channel that is timbre matched to your existing speakers. If your front speakers aren't timbre matched, transition effects will be noticeable and will take away from the realism of your home theater system. Because front-to-back sound transitions are not as common, you can use nontimbre matched speakers in the front and back. Although this setup is not optimal, it is certainly viable.

STEREO VS. MONO VCRS

A stereo VCR has two audio outputs—a right and a left; a mono VCR only has one sound output. A stereo VCR provides better overall sound and allows Dolby Pro Logic playback on material encoded with that surround sound format.

Establish Your Priorities

Think for a second about your ultimate home theater. Do you see a huge television? Maybe some incredible floor-standing speakers? Individual preferences are a key factor in deciding how to "divvy up" the budget. Do you want to spend a large portion of your budget buying that magnificent, big-screen television, or take advantage of your current television while building a sound system to be envied? Is big, theater sound more important than a huge television monitor? Does watching sporting events on a huge television monitor excite you more than incredible sound? Is shaking the pictures off the wall your only concern? You need to establish which items of your home theater system are to be more heavily weighed in the budget.

We will now build two hypothetical systems. One system puts more emphasis on the audio portion of the system; the other puts more emphasis on the video aspect of the system. Keep in mind that both systems stay within our $3,000 budget.

Both systems include the following home theater components:

- ▶ Television monitor
- ▶ Home theater receiver
- ▶ Five satellite speakers
- ▶ Powered subwoofer
- ▶ DVD player

System A features an enhanced audio portion of the home theater system. A system that is more "audio weighted" consists of high-quality speakers and a more-than-capable subwoofer. With this system, we spend the largest portion of the $3,000 budget on audio components. We dedicate approximately $2,000 of the total budget to the audio portions of System A. This

$2,000 covers the cost of the five satellite speakers, a powered subwoofer, and a home theater receiver. The remaining $1,000 covers the cost of the television monitor and DVD player. In Table 5.1, you can see the components and their respective prices that make up System A.

Table 5.1
System A—System with Audio Emphasis

Component	Price	Notes
Home theater receiver	$500	16% of total budget, a very capable receiver can be found for this price
Five-speaker system	$1000	Over 33% of total budget, speakers last for years
Powered subwoofer	$400	Can be the difference-maker in a home theater system
Television monitor	$600	Quality 32-inch television can be found for this price
DVD player	$200	Prices have plummeted and quality has increased

As you can see, System A has shaped up nicely, and also weighs heavily on audio—we've spent almost $2,000 on the audio portions of this system. You may also notice we've spent only $2,700 total. This is because we allowed 10% of our budget to cover minor expenses, such as remote controls, speaker stands, wires, and cabling. These items are often forgotten and can push your system over budget if not accounted for beforehand.

System B focuses on the video aspects of the home theater. Obviously, a large television is the focal point of this system and consumes a large portion of the budget. Because we use more budget money for the television monitor, the audio system is assembled with a smaller budget than in System A. Again, we save 10% of the total budget for various smaller costs associated with building a system. Table 5.2 displays the components and respective prices that make up System B.

Table 5.2
System B—System with Video Emphasis

Component	Price	Notes
Television monitor	$1600	Large percentage of budget to accommodate for big-screen television
Home theater receiver	$300	10% of total budget, but capable performers can be found for this price
Five-speaker system	$450	Smaller speaker system, but bigger video effects
Powered subwoofer	$150	Good budget subwoofers can be found in this price range
DVD player	$200	Prices have plummeted and quality has increased

By this point, you've probably developed a preference for either System A or System B. Both systems have advantages and disadvantages. System A can easily be upgraded by adding a large television monitor when your budget allows. System B features a television that will be around for many years and an audio system that can be upgraded as new technology is developed. Both systems can make use of existing components if and when you choose to upgrade to new surround sound formats. If the idea of eventually developing a projector-based theater room is appealing, System A should seem more attractive.

My Ideal Budget Home Theater System

Managing a budget home theater review website has allowed me ample opportunity to test and compare lots of equipment. Fortunately, I've been able to find some real gems in budget home theater components. I've also had the opportunity to help assemble numerous budget systems and listen to feedback on the individual components as well as on the system as a whole.

I've developed a "favorite" $3,000 budget system, based on all my research and experience with various setups. Included in this system are some spending percentages that give you an idea of how much you should spend on each component. Table 5.3 shows these estimates.

Table 5.3
Estimated Spending Percentages

Component	Percentage	Dollar Amount	Notes
Television	20%	$600	Allows for a nice 32-inch television
DVD player	7%	$200	Dropping prices allow you to find a DVD player with a great feature set
Receiver	13%	$400	The first area on which to spend more if your budget allows
Speaker set with subwoofer	50%	$1500	Half of the budget, but greatly impacts overall experience
Cables, stands, remotes	10%	$300	The final touches always cost more than expected

You should note a few things about Table 5.3. First, I assume you have an existing, workable VCR and don't need to purchase a new one. Also note that I've included the powered subwoofer within the cost of the speaker system. Many times, you can get package deals that offer discounts when purchasing a full 5.1 speaker setup.

Your initial reaction to the percentages given in Table 5.3 might be that it's crazy to spend half your budget on speakers alone. In my opinion, this couldn't be further from the truth. Speakers, especially the powered subwoofer, are usually the difference between a good system and an incredible system. Good amplification is also very important, but if you start with a good set of speakers, they only sound better when you upgrade to better amplification.

You may also note that the recommended spending percentages closely resemble System A, in which the audio is emphasized (see Table 5.1). My personal preference is a system that weighs heavier on audio than video. I've found that most people are looking to add home theater sound to their existing large television monitor rather than looking to add a large television to an existing home theater sound system. Also, upgrading to a larger television is much easier than upgrading to a new audio system, because you only have to buy one component (the TV). Another reason to put off the purchase of a big screen television is the fact that HDTV standards are still evolving.

Already own a television and DVD player? If so, you can either increase spending on other components or save the money to purchase your favorite movies and calibration discs. If you do decide to increase spending, the first area to consider upgrading is the home theater receiver. The receiver is an integral part of home theater performance, and by upgrading the receiver, you can obtain more advanced features, such as On Screen Display or component video switching— features that help keep your receiver from becoming outdated too quickly. After the receiver, you might consider a personal television recorder to record broadcast television programming.

Don't Forget the Extras

This section helps you remember to factor in the little things that can push your system over budget. Many people forget that when building a system, they must purchase smaller items, such as speaker wire, cables, and even speaker stands.

Speaker Wire and Interconnect Cables

For a five-speaker surround system, you need five speaker wires of various lengths. Speaker wire ranges from very inexpensive wire that can be found at your local hardware store to very expensive audiophile wire that costs several hundred dollars. For most budget home theater systems, inexpensive cable is just fine. I recommend buying twelve gauge speaker wire, as it provides good, all-around performance and is reasonably priced. Remember that these speaker cables may be much longer than anticipated because you should route the wires in a manner they can best be concealed. Surround speakers especially require long lengths of speaker cable. If possible, the preferred solution is routing the surround speaker wires through the wall. An easy way to tell if it is possible to run speaker wires in the wall is to look at the way cable television has been routed. If your cable television is in your attic and is dropped down the wall to an outlet, you can probably run speaker wire in the same fashion. If that is not a possibility, you may consider buying flat speaker wire that can be concealed under carpet.

Although your DVD player may come with cables, you probably want to buy an aftermarket cable to assure the best picture quality. Even the cheaper aftermarket cables commonly found at local electronics store provide a better picture and reduce the ghosting effects found in cheap cables that are provided with most home theater components. The included cables are typically very poor quality with minimal shielding, which introduces distortion and interference. Higher-quality cables feature quad shielding that can help minimize unwanted interference, especially when the cable is running close to a power cord. You also need several pairs of interconnects to connect your DVD player, VCR, and other devices into your receiver. After you've decided on your home theater components, it is a good idea to draw a diagram depicting the cables that provide audio and video connections among devices.

Speaker Stands

If you are buying bookshelf speakers, you'll need some sort of stands for them. You'll want to buy a stand that brings the speaker up to ear level. Speaker stands can be found for as little as $50 all the way up to over $200 for a pair. High-end stands often have features that allow the stand to make better connections with the floor and minimize resonance. Also, some stands can be filled with sand or other materials to give the stand a sturdier stance.

Entertainment Centers

Have you given any thought to where you are going to put all this new equipment? If you don't have a TV stand or an entertainment center, you'll probably need one for your new system. Entertainment centers and component racks can cost several hundred dollars, so be sure to budget for that accordingly. Entertainment centers have the advantage of being an "all-in-one" unit, as opposed to component racks, which have to be paired with some sort of television stand in most cases. Entertainment centers are typically more inexpensive than component racks. However, component racks do have some advantages over entertainment centers. Home theater components can become very warm during heavy use, and component racks often feature much better ventilation than entertainment centers. Also, component racks are a perfect complement to large, rear projection television sets that do not need a television stand.

If you opt to purchase a component rack instead of an entertainment center, a major feature to look for is cable management. Many component racks feature advanced ways to organize and group cables to tidy up the appearance, such as a channel that runs vertically up the back of the component rack. This vertical channel consists of a mechanism to help group cables that carry audio and video signals and keep them away from power cables. Running speaker wires and interconnects parallel to power cables can introduce unwanted interference. The interference—typically a humming sound—can be caused by alternating current electricity, which is found in all households.

Calibration Hardware and Software

After you get your system up and running, you need to calibrate it properly to achieve the highest level of performance. To do this correctly, you need a decibel meter and a calibration disc. A good calibration disc costs $40, but an acceptable disc can be found for under $20. A decibel meter (shown in Figure 5.1) typically costs around $30, so be sure to plan for these two added expenses.

Figure 5.1
A decibel meter
helps balance the
sound output from
your speakers

In Chapter 9, we explore the calibration process and explain it in more detail. Audio calibration involves using a DVD that has prerecorded sounds on it that aid you in obtaining an equal output on each speaker regardless of acoustic conditions in your room. Calibration not only helps achieve maximum audio performance, these calibration DVDs can also be used to adjust your television monitor to achieve truer colors. Calibration discs are especially important for rear projection television owners, as a properly-calibrated monitor is much less likely to suffer screen burn-in than an improperly-calibrated television monitor.

Universal Remote Controls

To enjoy your home theater system, all your components have to work together. The key to this is using a good universal remote control that can control all your devices. Universal remote controls are stand-alone units that have the ability to control various components in your home theater system. These remotes are often used to control different components from different manufacturers that use different remotes. Using a universal remote can help you get rid of the five remotes that came with various components in your system, and use only the single universal remote to control all the audio and video components in your system. Universal remotes have preprogrammed codes that you can use to gain access to all your components.

Many universal remotes have the ability to perform macros. Macros are a series of steps that can be programmed onto a single button. For instance, a macro could be created that turns on your television, receiver, DVD player, and VCR with the push of a single button. Macros often make controlling a complicated home theater system much easier than trying to perform a series of complicated remote control commands for common tasks.

There are thousands of universal remotes on the market. At the low end of functionality and price, there are the $20 remotes that offer basic feature replication of a limited set of components. If you've got a simple system, most likely you can get by with a cheaper universal remote, such as the Radio Shack 15-1994 shown in Figure 5.2. On the opposite end of the spectrum, there are high-tech, virtually limitless programmable remotes such as the Philip's Pronto, shown in Figure 5.3.

Figure 5.2
A great remote for a budget home theater system, the Radio Shack 15-1994 is a bargain at $30

If your system is a big, complex system full of many components, you probably need to budget for a more capable universal remote than the basic $20 variety found at the local electronics superstore. Many of these remotes hook into your home computer, and allow you to design a custom layout. These remotes have an almost unlimited potential to control huge systems and perform advanced operations.

Figure 5.3
The Philips Pronto is a sophisticated liquid crystal display (LCD) remote control

CHAPTER 5

Demo Material

Make sure your budget allows you to purchase your favorite movies on DVD. That's why you have a home theater system after all, isn't it? You'll want to be able to pull out great demo material when friends and family sit down to witness your new system for the first time. The following list provides some great discs to demonstrate the power of your new system. These discs help showcase the stellar power of your system in both incredible audio and superb video images.

▶ Toy Story 2: Stunning animation with a wide variety of great audio.

▶ Saving Private Ryan: Makes you feel like you are part of the storming of the beach at Normandy.

▶ U571: Depth charges make great subwoofer-testing material.

▶ Star Wars Episode I: The Phantom Menace: Great sound and video and includes an incredible THX trailer.

▶ The Matrix: The DVD that seemed to kick start the home theater trend.

▶ Shrek: A DTS soundtrack and video images that are second to none.

By planning for often forgotten items, like entertainment stands and cables, and allocating your budget properly, you can build a home theater system without breaking the bank. In the next chapter, you learn what to look for when you begin to shop for your components.

6

Selecting the Right Equipment

Most people don't have too many problems identifying the components that make up a home theater system—televisions, DVD players, and speakers have become synonymous with the term "home theater." However, a much smaller percentage of people can tell you what to look for when selecting that equipment. Although preference is often subjective, there are features and qualities that can be measured quantitatively.

When shopping for home theater gear, you'll be bombarded by marketing and buzzwords. If you aren't careful, you may end up paying too much for the wrong components. This chapter helps you choose the right equipment. By knowing what to look for when shopping, you'll be able to stretch your dollars and maximize your overall home theater experience.

At some point, you've probably shopped for a television set. Perhaps you can even tell a friend some important features to look for in televisions, but if that same friend asks you to pick out a powered subwoofer, can you do the same? Should you buy the all-in-one solution or purchase the same brand for all components? Let's answer these and other equipment-purchasing questions.

Selecting a Television Set

If you opt to purchase a new television for your home theater system, do you know what to look for? As described in Chapter 4, televisions come in hundreds of shapes, sizes, and prices. By breaking down the different choices in sets, you can make your decision much more easily.

Choosing the Right Display Technology

When buying a television set, the biggest decision is selecting the type of technology to be used. Are you drawn to the large size and adjustability of an RPTV? Or, would you rather stick with the more conventional CRT tube-based television that provides ease of use and years of trouble-free operation? By narrowing your choice of television technology, you can greatly simplify your choice.

If you are considering an RPTV, answer the following questions to make sure it is the right type of television for you.

▶ Do you like to "tweak" things to achieve maximum performance?

▶ Is watching DVD movies a bigger concern than watching television programming?

▶ Are you considering an HDTV set?

▶ Is having a wide-screen aspect ratio (16:9) important?

▶ Are you looking for a 40-inch or larger television set?

If you answered yes to the majority of the previous questions, then an RPTV is probably the right choice for you. The most decisive question is the one about size. If you are considering a set over 40 inches in diagonal length, then an RPTV is not only the right answer; it's basically the only option.

RPTV sets do not have an optimal picture when you first take them out of the box. The alignment of the three-color guns is not optimal, and the set needs to run about 100 hours before the internal components settle in. To achieve an optimal picture on an RPTV, you have to take some time and effort to correct the initial problems.

With most RPTV sets, after 100 hours of normal use, the set has settled enough that the convergence (alignment of the red, green, and blue light guns) of the set can be corrected and the correction will be close to permanent. Over time, the convergence may drift a small amount, but unless you move the set, it should stay accurate.

If you plan to purchase a high-definition monitor, an RPTV is usually the more cost-effective route. For watching DVD playback, a wide-screen (16:9 aspect ratio) RPTV is tough to beat. Many DVDs are enhanced specifically for playback on wide-screen television sets. These DVDs take advantage of the high resolution, as the wide-screen format allows for 33 percent more vertical resolution—providing a better picture.

If you plan to purchase a wide-screen television set but still want to watch broadcast television, ensure that you are comfortable watching a "stretched" picture. Normal television programming uses a 4:3 aspect ratio. A wide-screen television (1.78:1 aspect ratio) is wider than standard programming (1.33:1 aspect ratio). The result is that you either have to watch programming stretched or watch the programming with black (or gray) bars to fill the empty space. Most wide-screen televisions offer several types of stretch modes to fit your individual preference. Some of these modes stretch the image uniformly across the screen, whereas others stretch the edges of the image more than they stretch the center.

You can see the stretching effect in Figure 6.1. To fill the entire screen, the image must be stretched, thus distorting it from its original format. Some people don't notice the stretched picture at all, and it drives others crazy. Before you purchase an RPTV, make sure you find the solutions acceptable.

Figure 6.1
Wide-screen television sets stretch standard television programming to fill the larger viewing area

If you do decide that a wide-screen television is the right solution for you, make sure you understand aspect ratio. Many people are very surprised to learn that when watching DVDs on a wide-screen television, there are still black bars at the top and bottom of the screen. (See Figure 6.2.) Often, the 16:9 (1.78:1) aspect ratio of HDTV is confused with the even wider aspect ratios common in movies, which are shot at anywhere from 1.85:1 to 2.35:1.

Figure 6.2
Even with 16:9 aspect ratios, wide-screen televisions still have black bars when watching some DVDs

CHAPTER 6

Movies are shot in a variety of aspect ratios. The most typical ratios are the previously mentioned 1.85:1 and 2.35:1. A wide-screen television possesses a 1.78:1 aspect ratio. As you can see, the DVD's aspect ratio is even wider than a wide-screen television. The black bars on a wide-screen television are much smaller than the black bars you see when watching the same movie on a television with a conventional aspect ratio.

Let's compare watching a 2.35:1 aspect ratio movie on a wide-screen television and a standard television (1:33.1 aspect ratio). The wide-screen television has a total viewing area (actual image, not counting black bars) over 16 percent larger than the standard aspect ratio television. Figure 6.3 illustrates this point.

Figure 6.3
Compare the differences in the black bars between a wide-screen and standard television

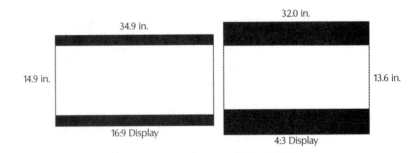

In Figure 6.3, you can see the differences in black bars on a 40-inch wide-screen set and a 40-inch standard television set. The wide-screen set has only 4.7 total inches of black bars, whereas the standard set has 10.4 total inches of black bars. The dimensions of the total viewing area on the wide-screen set are 14.9 inches × 34.9 inches. The dimensions of the total viewing area on the standard set are 13.6 inches × 32.0 inches. As you can see, wide-screen televisions offer a significantly greater viewing area than a standard aspect ratio television.

If you think a more conventional CRT tube-based television is what you are looking for, consider the following questions.

▶ Do you prefer your television to be functional right out of the box?

▶ Do you watch more television programming than DVD movies?

▶ Are size and space big factors in your purchase?

▶ Are you planning on buying a 40-inch or smaller television set?

If you are looking for an immediate, low-maintenance solution, then a conventional CRT tube-based television is most likely the proper choice. CRT tube-based televisions provide very good pictures from the moment they are turned on. Most often, little work is required from a CRT tube-based television to achieve maximum picture quality.

If you plan to buy a set that is 40 inches or smaller, CRT tube-based televisions are the best option. However, remember to consider the cost of a stand or armoire to raise the television to eye level. Also, remember that the flat display monitors, like the Sony Wega, are considerably more expensive than sets with a curved front glass panel.

Currently, almost all CRT tube-based television sets have a 4:3 (standard) aspect ratio. There are some high-definition ready tube televisions that have the wide-screen 16:9 aspect ratio, but they are not common at this point. If you want the ease of a tube television but prefer the increased viewing area on DVD playback, buying a CRT wide-screen television is a viable option. Again, remember that standard television programming has to be stretched to fit the wide-screen television.

If you've decided to go with the conventional CRT tube-based television, but you don't like having to give up the added vertical resolution the wide-screen format gives you, there is an option. Some high-end 4:3 television sets have a feature called "anamorphic squeeze" that allows standard television sets to take advantage of the 33 percent greater resolution on the 16:9 enhanced DVDs. This feature is also referred to as "vertical compression" or "16:9 Enhanced Mode." Television sets that have this advanced feature make use of the otherwise unused extra vertical resolution available on wide-screen enhanced discs.

Features to Look For

Regardless of the display technology, there are certain features that you should look for when selecting a television. CRT, rear projection, and plasma display devices all benefit from added inputs and picture-in-picture display.

As discussed in the DVD player section of Chapter 5, there are many types of audio and video connections to link your components (see Figure 6.4). The best connection is component video. You'll also want to ensure that your television set has several S-Video inputs for those devices that don't feature component video. Don't forget, though, that, if needed, your receiver can help with a shortage of inputs by performing the video switching for the television.

Figure 6.4
A television's input panel featuring component, S-Video, and composite inputs

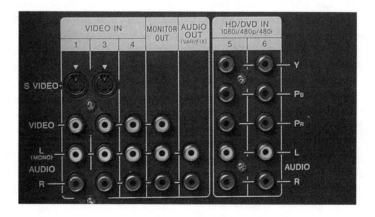

Picture-in-picture (PIP) display is a feature that allows you to watch another program in a small window while continuing to watch another full-screen program. This feature allows you to channel surf during commercial breaks while keeping an eye on your original program. Some televisions feature two-tuner PIP. This allows you to watch two different programs without using an external tuning device, such as a VCR.

Selecting the Right DVD Player

DVD players have quickly become a regular household item, but with prices ranging from $80 to over $2,000, selecting the right one is often difficult. This section helps identify the crucial features to look for when selecting the right DVD player. In addition, we help you get the correct DVD player to complement your television monitor.

The first decision is whether to buy a single-disc player or a multiple-disc carousel unit. Single-disc players are more common and also cheaper than a similarly-equipped multiple-disc unit. Multiple-disc units, boasting from 5 to over 300-disc capability, allow you to have access to many discs without having to physically change the disc out. For most budget home theaters, a single-disc unit is fine.

The second major decision is whether to spend the extra money for a DVD player that can output progressive scan. If you have, or plan to buy soon, a television monitor capable of displaying the 480p signal, then you should give serious consideration to buying a progressive scan player. Progressive scan provides a smoother image, with fewer motion artifacts.

If you do decide to buy a progressive scan player, make sure you buy a player that has a 2:3 pull-down feature, (also called 3:2 pull down). 2:3 pull down takes film material (24 frames per second) and converts it to a television format (60 frames per second). Most progressive scan players have this feature, but there are some models, such as the Pioneer DV434, that don't have it.

Whether you choose to buy a progressive or interlaced scan player, make sure that any DVD player you buy outputs both Dolby Digital and DTS bitstreams. There are a few players on the market that actually decode the digital surround sound bitstream, but if you plan to buy a home theater receiver, you won't need that feature.

Other less crucial but "nice to have" features include zoom, slow motion, and fast forward. Zoom allows you to zoom in on the picture on the screen to examine details. Slow motion is the ability to slow down the playback to watch fast action more closely. Fast forward is the ability to speed up the playback in high multiples—allowing for quick access to specific areas of the disc. Most players offer several multiples of fast forward and reverse.

Selecting the Right Receiver

The home theater receiver brings all your sights and sounds together and this plays an integral role in your system. That's why choosing the right receiver is most important. Receivers range in price from $200 to well over $5,000. There are many capable receivers on the market, and this section helps you distinguish features that are absolutely necessary from those that are fun but not essential.

Amplification and Features

The most important function of the receiver is its ability to amplify signals and reproduce sound. The receiver you purchase should be capable of producing acceptable volume levels without distorting the sound too much. Larger rooms need more amplification, but a good starting point is to find a receiver rated at 70 watts per channel over the entire spectrum (20

Hz–20,000 Hz) with less than .1% distortion. This information should be readily available, so be sure to ask the salesperson if you don't see it. Alternatively, you can look up the manufacturer's web page to inquire about the specifications of the receiver.

Another crucial feature of a home theater receiver is the ability to decode Dolby Digital and DTS bitstreams. Your DVD player provides the digital bitstream from the DVD disc, but your receiver is responsible for decoding that disc and reproducing the appropriate sounds. Almost all receivers sold today feature both Dolby Digital and DTS decoding.

Some newer and more expensive receivers may also feature Dolby Digital EX or DTS ES decoding. These surround sound formats build off Dolby Digital and DTS formats and offer six or seven channels of surround sound. This feature, however, is not that common in budget theaters today. If you plan to upgrade to a six- or seven-channel surround sound system in the future, you should consider buying a receiver that will process these two newer surround sound formats.

Most receivers feature an array of DSP sound fields. DSP stands for digital signal processing, and is a way to alter the sound characteristics of an original source. Most of these DSP sound fields are designed to simulate different venues, such as an auditorium or concert hall. Although these features are nice, most have little or no practical use.

Home theater receivers usually come with a universal remote control that is capable of "learning" codes from other remote controls; a universal remote simplifies your control of your home theater system. If the receiver you are purchasing doesn't have a quality universal remote control, be sure to buy one.

Your receiver outputs sound to your speakers. To ensure the best connections and minimize interference and signal loss, make sure to select a receiver that uses binding posts for all speaker connections. Signal loss is losing information from the original source signal, resulting in lower-quality sound. For more information, see the "Connections" section later in this chapter.

Inputs and Video Switching

The receiver receives audio and video signals from all devices in your home theater. So, you want to make sure your receiver has enough inputs to cover all your components. Budget receivers typically have many composite video inputs and several S-Video inputs, but often lack component video inputs. However, the lack of component inputs can be overcome. If your television has component inputs, you can simply run the video signal straight into the television, and route the audio signal to the receiver. Because component video allows the best connection, it is often preferred to run the video source straight to the television to reduce signal degradation and maximize picture quality.

An increasingly important feature in home theater receivers is the number of digital inputs. DVD players, satellite dish receivers, and even video game systems use digital connections to home theater receivers to take advantage of the clean digital sound. There are two types of digital connections: optical and coaxial. Make sure the receiver you select has at least four total digital inputs.

Video switching is the ability of your receiver, a typically audio-oriented device, to accept multiple video signals and select which video source is output to the television. If your television has only one S-Video input, but you have several S-Video sources, you can use your receiver to handle the switching of these sources.

Selecting the Right Speakers

The speaker system you select has a profound impact on the sound of your home theater system. Speaker preference is very subjective, and each person has to decide for himself what sounds best. However, there are features and characteristics to look for when shopping for speakers.

For a true home theater experience, you need at least five separate speakers and a powered subwoofer. But will just any speakers do? Obviously, with the incredibly wide range of speaker prices, all speakers are not created equal.

Sensitivity, Resistance, and Power

Speakers are rated on a variety of parameters. Each speaker is rated for sensitivity. Sensitivity is how much sound, measured in decibels, the speaker produces when given one watt of power. The higher this rating, the more efficient the speaker is. Look for a sensitivity rating around 90 db. Efficient speakers require less power than inefficient speakers to reach the same volume levels.

Speakers are also rated on their average resistance. Most home theater speakers offer an average resistance of eight ohms. A lower resistance rating, for instance six ohms, presents a higher resistance level for your receiver. This can result in more power, but also results in your receiver being pushed harder. Resistance ratings between four and eight ohms are acceptable for use with most budget home theater receivers.

Often, speakers also carry a rating specification about the maximum amount of watts that should be used in conjunction with the speaker. This rating should simply be used to ensure that you aren't going to overpower your speakers with too much amplification. Most often, your receiver's power output is well within the range of the speaker's recommended amplification level. Don't worry if the receiver's power output is close to the maximum that your speakers can handle; speakers are more easily harmed by the distortion present at high volume levels from a low power receiver than from a high-powered receiver pushing too much power through them.

Frequency Range

A more meaningful rating, one that is helpful in deciding on a speaker, is frequency range. Frequency range is the range of sounds, rated in hertz (Hz), that the speaker is capable of producing. Different types of speakers have different frequency responses. For instance, a floor-standing speaker with larger drivers most likely has a better low-end frequency response than a smaller bookshelf speaker.

TYPICAL FREQUENCY RESPONSE RATINGS

A typical frequency response rating for a speaker looks something like the following:

Frequency response 85–25,000 Hz (±3dB)

The ±3dB means that the speaker's response across the stated range of frequencies may vary from the ideal as much as 3 dB. This is a typical range; greater deviations, of 4, 5, or 6 dB, for instance, indicate less accurate frequency response.

In an ideal world, you want all your speakers to be able to reproduce sounds from 20 Hz to 20,000 Hz. This means that each speaker is capable of reproducing the entire audible frequency range. Realistically, this doesn't happen. In real-world applications, look for frequency responses lower than 80 Hz and higher than 20,000 Hz.

Most of the time, speakers can hit the 20,000 Hz response criteria, so you'll typically be more concerned with a speaker's low-frequency rating. This rating dictates how well the speaker reproduces bass frequencies, the ones that create the earth-shaking sounds. Remember that your primary speakers have the aid of a powered subwoofer to re-create sounds below 80 Hz, so it isn't mission critical that they be able to respond much below 80 Hz.

Connections

As mentioned in the receiver section, a good connection from the receiver to the speaker wire is essential for achieving interference-free sound. Just as important is the connection from the speaker wire to the speaker. Just like the receiver, speakers that use binding posts are preferred.

Binding posts are often called "5-way binding posts." This is a way of denoting the multiple connection options that are possible with binding posts. Binding posts allow for better connections than spring-loaded clips and offer greater versatility by allowing various methods of connections. Spring-loaded clips are usually limited to bare wire or pin-speaker connections. Binding posts allow the use of bare wire, spade connectors, and banana plugs. (See Figure 6.5.)

Figure 6.5
Binding posts offer solid connections to help minimize interference and distortion

CHAPTER 6

Matching Speakers

The most important thing to remember when purchasing home theater speakers is to always match your speakers. This doesn't necessarily mean that you have to use identical speakers for left, right, and center channels, but it does mean to make sure that all three of your front speakers have the same tonal characteristics. This is often referred to as timbre matching.

Movies frequently include sounds that start on one side of the screen and move to the opposite side of the screen. As the action pans across the screen, the sound pans across the three front speakers. If the tonal characteristics of these speakers are not the same, an audible difference is heard as the sound transitions.

Speaker manufacturers realize this need for similar-sounding speakers. They've addressed this need by selling matching center channels that share tonal characteristics with their left and right channels. Sometimes, the center channel is the exact same speaker as the left and right, which guarantees seamless transitions. Figure 6.6 shows an example of this.

Figure 6.6
It is essential to buy timbre matched left, right, and center speakers, like these Aperion Audio speakers

So, how do you know if speakers are timbre matched? The easiest way to determine this is to listen to "pink noise" tests on a calibration DVD, such as Avia. Pink noise resembles the sound of static, but it is actually a sound that contains all the audible frequencies that a human can hear. When played, pink noise helps identify transition problems.

If space allows, having five identical speakers surrounding the listening area certainly provides smooth transitions. As stated in Chapter 3, although it is important to timbre match your front and rear speakers as well, it is not as critical as matching the front three speakers.

Speaker Components

A typical bookshelf speaker consists of two components, a tweeter and a woofer. The tweeter is a small speaker that reproduces high-frequency sounds. The woofer is a much larger component that reproduces bass and mid-range frequencies. These two components work together to reproduce all the sounds of the audible range.

Tweeters

The tweeter component of speakers can be further categorized into different types of tweeters. Typical tweeter types are horn and dome. These two types have different dispersion characteristics. The horn tweeter focuses its sound dispersion and increases its efficiency and output. The dome tweeter has a wide dispersion area but is not as efficient as the horn tweeter.

Although they offer some advantages, few modern speakers feature horn tweeters. In fact, Klipsch is one of the few brands that still uses horn tweeters in its speakers. If horn tweeters are so efficient, why don't more people use them? Due to their focused sound and efficiency, horn tweeters have a very forward, often called bright, sound presentation. This brightness can be fatiguing to some people's ears, hence many people choose dome tweeters.

Woofers

Most speakers' woofer components look very similar. However, the main difference usually revolves around the material from which the woofer is made. Common woofers are constructed from aluminum and paper. Paper woofer cones are more common in lower-end budget speakers, whereas more expensive alloy cones are often found in high-end applications.

When shopping for speakers, look for a woofer that is at least 6 1/2 inches in diameter. This size woofer is big enough to produce frequencies below 80 Hz. As mentioned previously, alloy cones are typically preferable to paper cones, but each individual application differs.

Selecting the Right Powered Subwoofer

To re-create those room-rattling explosions and thunderous steps from the dinosaur, a powered subwoofer is absolutely necessary (see Figure 6.7). The powered subwoofer, often an unseen component of the home theater, focuses on limited frequency reproduction. A typical subwoofer re-creates the small frequency range between 20 Hz and 80 Hz.

Figure 6.7
Powered subwoofers, like this Aperion Audio SW8, create house-shaking low frequencies

Subwoofers usually feature a single, large-diameter woofer. Typical sizes for powered subwoofers are eight, ten, and twelve inches in diameter. These woofers are contained in an enclosure that is either sealed or ported. Ported enclosures have port holes that allow sound from inside the enclosure to escape, making them more efficient and louder. Sealed enclosures are air tight, which makes them more accurate but they usually need more amplification.

Subwoofers are deemed "powered" if they contain an integrated amplifier. Amplifier power ratings generally range from 100 watts to over 500 watts. Because subwoofers are often hidden in corners, the amplifiers commonly feature automatic on/off features. When the unit senses a signal, it powers on and stays on until a set amount of time has passed without a signal, then the unit powers off.

Subwoofers typically feature variable crossovers. A crossover allows only certain frequencies to pass through, eliminating other frequencies. Because a subwoofer only reproduces a small range, a low-pass crossover is used to only allow frequencies below a set point to pass through. A variable crossover is a crossover that can be set at any point on the scale. A typical crossover range on a powered subwoofer is 20 Hz to 150 Hz. For example, if the crossover is set to 75 Hz, only frequencies equal to or lower than 75 Hz are sent to the subwoofer.

Subwoofers connect to your receiver via the subwoofer output jack. This output is the ".1" in a "5.1" surround sound system. An RCA connection is the easiest and most effective way to connect the subwoofer. Most subwoofers also have speaker-level inputs available, but these inputs should be used only if you do not have a dedicated subwoofer output on your receiver.

NOTE
Only receivers that are not Dolby Digital-compliant lack a dedicated subwoofer output. If your receiver has Dolby Pro Logic Surround, but not Dolby Digital, then you will not have a dedicated subwoofer output. In this case, you need to use the speaker level inputs.

Powered subwoofers are often an expensive component of the home theater system. For most budget systems, look for a ten- or twelve-inch woofer with at least 125 watts of power to drive the woofer. Most have similar features, so often performance is the deciding factor. Be warned that room placement is a critical factor in subwoofer performance. If at first you aren't pleased with your subwoofer's performance, try different locations. Often placing a subwoofer in a corner, called corner loading, results in much louder playback.

Now that you know what features and characteristics to look for in home theater components, the next chapter helps you maximize your budget when shopping.

7

Shopping for Your System

Shopping for home theater components can be overwhelming. After you've selected which sorts of components you'd like to purchase, you then have to decide where to buy them. Should you buy online to save money? Can you trust the faceless store on the Internet to provide customer service if something goes wrong? Should you instead buy locally to get great face-to-face service if the need arises? Tough choices like these make many shoppers grow weary.

In this chapter, we compare buying online versus buying from a local merchant. We also help you learn secrets to maximizing your money. For instance, should you buy an "open box" or a "close-out" receiver? This chapter answers that question and many more.

The Internet provides a wealth of information for those looking to build a home theater. Reviews, ratings, technical specifications, and prices for all home theater components are on the web. Thousands of online merchants have a minimal overhead and sell large quantities of components at reduced prices.

Another recent development via the Internet is the invention of "direct to the consumer" manufacturers. Often dubbed DTCs, these manufacturers have effectively cut out the retailer. You won't find their no-name products at your local audio and video superstore, but you may find that their products outperform those name brands you do find at your local store—and at a much lower cost. We explore DTCs later in the chapter.

Last, we explore common shopping dilemmas you could encounter. Should you buy the same brand for all of your components? Should you buy last year's closeout model or a demo? What about refurbished goods? We clear up the confusion on all these subjects and help you identify which bargains you should go after and which ones to avoid.

Local Merchants

Most people simply go down to their local audio/video store to purchase new home theater components. Local merchants obviously offer in-person customer service and the opportunity to sample a variety of brands and models firsthand. However, due to the higher overhead associated with running a local store, the local merchant's prices are often high. Let's examine the pros and cons of buying locally.

Advantages of Buying Locally

Most people looking to build a new home theater system have a limited knowledge of the components they need. Local merchants often have a knowledgeable sales staff who listen to your needs and help steer you toward equipment that suits your needs. Local shops also tend to have a wide selection of material in stock, so you can physically compare the look, feel, and performance of each item.

Your local retailer should also provide that extra assistance when you run into trouble. If you purchased an entire system from your local retailer, he is likely to help you with connections, setup, and other pertinent and potential difficulties. However, if you purchased all your new gear on the Internet and run into problems, online retailers are less likely to assist you after the initial product purchase.

Local retailers also sometimes invite customers to take equipment and test it in their home environment before buying. Because every room is unique and offers a different acoustic signature, taking advantage of this testing opportunity can prove invaluable—it allows you to determine if the more expensive receiver provides enough of a difference in your own home to justify buying it instead of the less expensive model.

Although most local retailers display the manufacturer's suggested retail price (MSRP), most are willing to negotiate. Don't expect your local dealer to match the Internet price, but it never hurts to inquire about the possibility of obtaining the product at a lower than suggested price. The ticketed price isn't always set in stone. Keep in mind that because they have been hurt by Internet retailers, local merchants rely on their ability to provide quality customer support before and after the sale. And they may even sacrifice some profit by lowering their prices.

Your local dealer may be inclined to offer a substantial discount if you purchase several items from him. For example, you are more likely to get a discount if you buy a receiver, a five-speaker system, a powered subwoofer, and a DVD player than if you just buy a receiver. You may also be able to get your dealer to include cables, wires, and other extras.

If your home theater system requires an extensive installation, a local retailer has numerous advantages over an Internet retailer. A local retailer will most likely have an installation staff. Remember that you'll want your home theater to have a great appearance and a great sound, so finding a way to hide speaker wires and manage interconnect cables is essential. Your local retailer may be willing to help with your installation, often at a reduced rate, or perhaps even for free, if you buy your entire system from him.

One final big advantage to buying from your local retailer, especially if you're impatient, is that you get to walk out of the door with your purchase in hand. Even if you pay expensive overnight shipping from an Internet retailer, in most cases, you are still forced to wait at least twenty-four hours to get your new purchase. Keep in mind that home theater components often arrive in big, heavy boxes that add up to a hefty shipping charge.

Disadvantages of Buying Locally

Although your local merchant offers many advantages, there are also significant disadvantages you should consider before running out to buy your system. Obviously, local retailers incur much higher operation costs than Internet stores. A local store has to pay comparatively hefty real estate or rent prices. And the knowledgeable staff doesn't come free, either! You can see why local retailers charge higher prices for their products.

Price is obviously the biggest disadvantage to buying locally, but other disadvantages exist as well. Local retailers are open only a limited number of hours, which means you must shop during those hours. Internet shopping, on the other hand, can be done at any time. By shopping locally, you are also geographically limited to a relatively small number of audio/visual shops (compared to the large numbers of retailers online).

Internet Retailers

Internet shopping for home theater products is becoming commonplace. And for good reason. It opens up an enormous amount of freedom in shopping. You may not be able to find certain brands in your hometown shops, but you can find those brands online. Moreover, whereas your hometown likely has only a handful of audio/visual stores, the Internet allows you to compare prices and buy merchandise from retailers all over the world. This increased competition and information offers you power when making your buying decisions.

Advantages of Internet Shopping

Cost is often the most important factor when putting together a budget system, and Internet retailers just can't be beat when it comes to sheer price. Increased competition and low overhead allow online merchants to sell products at much lower prices than their local counterparts. For most online merchants, the rent is relatively low and the labor relatively cheap, as employees don't have to be knowledgeable experts, just order processors.

Many Internet retailers are simply "box shops." An online box shop is a web page run by a warehouse. Because the warehouse can be in an isolated location where real estate is inexpensive, the company's overhead is low. Low overhead translates into the box shop operations selling products for less money. Because these shops have a huge customer base on the Internet, they also have higher volumes that allow them to get better prices from manufacturers.

Internet shopping also enables you to shop on your schedule. You can shop via the Internet twenty-four hours a day, seven days a week—even on holidays. Plus, you don't have to deal with busy shopping malls, long waiting lines, and bad weather. In addition, there's no salesperson verbally pressuring you to buy now before you walk out the door. Did I mention that you save gas and wear and tear on your car too?

Another often overlooked advantage to shopping online is that most of your purchases are tax free. When you buy products online, you typically don't have to pay a local sales tax. Although this may not seem like a huge advantage, the savings really start to add up when you buy several thousand dollars' worth of equipment. Shopping tax free through the web might just give you the added savings you need to upgrade to a more expensive component than you could buy locally.

Finally, many online shops run blowout sales. If you've got the time to shop around and wait for a sale, you may find just the deal you are looking for. Also, you can often find coupon codes and special last-minute bargains that save you even more money.

Direct to the Consumer Manufacturers

Have you ever heard of Outlaw Audio (see Figure 7.1), Swan Divas, or Aperion Audio? If you are an avid home theater enthusiast who reads online magazines and frequents the home theater message boards, chances are you have. Such products aren't carried by most local retail establishments, but they have quickly become favorites with budget-minded Internet shoppers. These brands come from companies that are part of a new breed of retailers called "Direct to the Consumer" (DTC) manufacturers.

Figure 7.1
Outlaw Audio receivers
are a favorite on Internet
message boards

DTCs eliminate the "middle-man." By relying strictly on Internet sales, such companies bank on word-of-mouth. They have constructed home theater products that rival much higher priced name-brand equipment, but because they don't have the added overhead of selling in a showroom, they can offer their products at lower prices. See Figure 7.2.

Many DTCs offer risk-free trial periods. They realize that audio preferences differ from person to person, so they allow the customer to buy the product and try it at home. If after the trial period, the customer doesn't like the product, it can be returned for a full refund. Some DTCs even offer to pay for return shipping costs, providing a truly risk-free trial period. Although listening to products in a showroom is valuable, it can't match testing the system in your own home theater room.

Figure 7.2
The SW-12 powered subwoofer from Aperion Audio competes with much higher-priced subwoofers

CHAPTER 7

If you don't frequent home theater message boards on the Internet, you probably haven't given serious consideration to buying from an unknown manufacturer. Most shoppers unfamiliar with a product's brand simply ignore that product and opt for something from a familiar brand. I urge you to consider products from manufacturers you haven't heard of.

When I first discovered DTCs, I was skeptical. I liked the idea of buying directly from the manufacturer, but I didn't really think an upstart speaker company could produce anything worthy of a spot in my home theater. So I decided to contact some of these companies to arrange for review units. After testing the first set of speakers from a DTC, I was blown away, shocked at the incredible sound emanating from the speakers.

I was determined to prove that this wasn't a one-shot wonder, so I acquired several different speakers from multiple DTCs. I consistently found that DTCs were producing better speakers than the big-name brands.

I am now convinced that DTCs are the one of the best reasons for Internet shopping. In fact, the speakers I hand-picked for my home theater are from a DTC. I urge you to at least give DTC speaker shops a chance—I don't think you'll be disappointed.

Disadvantages of Internet Shopping

Many consumers are leery of Internet shopping. Stories of stolen credit cards, ordering mishaps, and nightmare returns tend to scare us, and rightfully so. Internet shopping is a very impersonal experience and has its drawbacks.

The most visible disadvantage to Internet shopping is high shipping costs. Home theater products, especially powered subwoofers and receivers, are typically large and heavy, which means shipping can be costly. Although ground-shipping rates are affordable, ground shipping can also be slow. Expect at least five working days to receive products.

Internet shopping doesn't offer much in the way of service. Of course, you'll get all the service in the world before you buy your components, but can you be sure that you'll continue to get the same service in nine months? Many Internet retailers aren't so good at helping customers after a sale is made. Also, problems with electronic components typically surface early in the component's life. Are you prepared to ship your brand-new component back to the retailer and then wait a few days for a new one to arrive? Will the retailer be willing to cooperate and help you get the matter resolved in a timely fashion? If you do decide to buy from an Internet retailer, find out the answers to these questions before you purchase anything.

Another downside to buying over the Internet is the plethora of unauthorized dealers and scammers. Companies such as Denon and Onkyo authorize their dealer networks; look for the "Authorized Dealer" logo displayed on the site. (See Figure 7.3.) If you buy from an unauthorized dealer, you may encounter problems should you have to send your component back to the manufacturer for repairs.

Some manufacturers don't approve the sale of their products via the Internet. You must buy their components from a qualified retailer. Therefore, you won't be able to buy every brand over the Internet. If you are looking for a particular brand and that brand is not available for purchase over the Internet, then you will have to buy that product from a local dealer.

Figure 7.3
Many manufacturers certify their dealers for online sales; be careful when selecting an Internet retailer

Ultimately, the decision to buy online or locally comes down to how much the security of buying locally means to you. Suppose you can get a receiver on the Internet from an authorized dealer for $100 less than your local dealer is willing to sell it to you. Is it worth the extra price to have the peace of mind that comes with buying locally? That is up to you to decide.

Shopping for Components

You made the decision to buy locally or via the Internet. Now comes the time to figure out what to buy. You need to ask yourself some important questions: Should you buy all of your components from the same manufacturer? Should you go for the closeout sale on last year's model? Is a refurbished receiver an option? Let's tackle these and other questions related to buying your home theater components.

Advantages of Buying Same Brand Components

Many home theater shoppers buy components manufactured by one company. For instance, someone who chooses to use the same, trusted manufacturer for all their components will buy a television monitor, DVD player, and receiver from the same brand. There are certain benefits to buying equipment from the same manufacturer that can outweigh the drawbacks.

The first noticeable advantage is that it makes remote control selection much easier. Most manufacturers include remotes already well-versed in controlling other devices from the same manufacturer. (See Figure 7.4.) For instance, a Sony television remote control should inherently control a Sony VCR and vice versa. For someone who is inexperienced in programming universal remote controls, this feature may be quite important, helpful, and even necessary.

FIGURE 7.4

Remote controls often offer the ability to control other devices from the same manufacturer

Manufacturers also tend to incorporate a similar look and feel throughout their product lines. It may be much easier for a novice user to operate a DVD player that operates and feels very similar to the VCR that he or she has used for years. You are not likely to find a common layout or feel when using remotes from different manufacturers. If you are concerned about being able to control all the components in your home theater system, buying components from the same manufacturer can decrease the complexity.

Disadvantages of Buying Same Brand Components

Although buying all your components from the same manufacturer can make using your system a breeze, there are some drawbacks. If you ask an expert, "Who makes the best home theater receivers and who makes the best television monitors?" you'll likely get the names of at least two different manufacturers. It isn't likely that a single manufacturer offers the best value and quality in a television monitor, a DVD player, and a home theater receiver.

I've found that you can increase the overall quality of your system by specializing your brand for each component. For instance, Toshiba offers great values in television sets, but they don't even manufacturer home theater receivers, so you should opt for a respected home theater receiver, such as something from Pioneer Elite, Onkyo, or Denon. This allows you to get a great television and home theater receiver—instead of getting a great television but only a mediocre receiver that just happened to be the same brand as your television. Brand loyalty is fine, but just make sure your loyalty doesn't keep you from getting a quality component.

Closeout Items

When building a budget home theater system, every dollar counts. If you can save money on a receiver, it may free up just enough budget space to get that more expensive television monitor you were eyeing. Closeout items can offer some great prices, but great prices don't necessarily translate into great buys. Before buying a closeout item, be sure to find out why the product is being discontinued.

If a manufacturer is discontinuing a product, a replacement for that product is in the works or already available. Before impulsively buying last year's model, make sure that the upcoming model doesn't offer significant upgrades that would be worth the extra money. Home theater products change to meet new standards and incorporate new innovations. A good example of this is Onkyo's recent product release. Onkyo established a firm hold on the budget home theater receiver market with the introduction of its TX-DS575X receiver. Many experts heralded this as the best receiver for under $500. When Onkyo discontinued the very popular 575X, it announced the TX-DS595, which added features such as Dolby Pro Logic II decoding. Many people who rushed out to buy closeout 575X receivers found they would have preferred to spend the extra money to get the DPL II decoding. That said, if the new model doesn't offer a significant improvement over the discontinued model, then a closeout model can be a great buy.

Refurbished Items

Refurbished components are another common shopping spot for bargain-hunting home theater consumers. Refurbished items are items that had some initial problem that was fixed by the factory. In theory, these products are exactly like a new product, because they've been repaired to the same specifications that the new products are built under. However, these products cannot be sold as new and are usually dubbed as refurbished.

Refurbished items are common in the electronics world, because if a unit has a problem, it typically surfaces early in the life of the product. These products get exchanged at a retail store and are then sent back to the manufacturer for repairs—and then, they are sent on to the refurbished shelf. Refurbished items are also commonly found on auction sites. Retailers are required to note that an item is refurbished. However, many retailers don't make it really clear that an item is refurbished—you really need to look for and read the fine print.

Refurbished items tend to be hit and miss. I've bought several refurbished items that have worked perfectly for years. However, I've also seen many problems with refurbished goods. Although theory says that they should have the same failure rate as a brand-new component, history shows that there tends to be a higher risk percentage associated with buying a refurbished product. If you are an adventurous shopper and don't mind taking a risk to save some money, refurbished products can be great deals. However, if you get peace of mind by minimizing the chances of dealing with nonworking components, you should probably avoid buying refurbished goods.

Auctions

Online auctions are another option for consumers looking for good deals. Auction sites, such as Ebay and Ubid, offer a gathering place for people looking to buy and sell merchandise in various conditions. Auction sites can offer good prices, but—as with Internet shopping—you increase your risk of running into a few hassles when trying to return a product that is not working properly, especially when buying from a lesser-known source. Auctions work in various ways, but the most popular is an auction between five and seven days where various buyers bid on the item.

Auction shopping can offer some great values, as you may find brand-new merchandise for sale. However, the process of auction shopping takes considerable more time and effort, because you're not just buying a product, you also have to keep track that you get a good deal and that you win the auction. Although an item will probably receive few bids early in the auction, as the auction closes, the action will surely increase. This requires that you monitor the auction, always checking the site, and rethinking how much you are willing to pay.

A common pitfall of online auction shopping is outrageous shipping charges. Some auction sites offer great bargains, but the bargains diminish quickly when you factor in unreasonably high shipping charges. Ubid.com in particular has very high shipping charges. They charge a base-shipping rate and then add on per pound. Home theater equipment is typically heavy, so the shipping charges escalate quickly. If you do find a good deal on an auction site, make sure you add the additional shipping costs into your figures to make sure that you are still saving money.

All things considered, though, there are good deals to be found on auction sites. If you have more time than money, auction sites may be a good fit for you. The worst mistake you can make is to rush into a decision. Take your time and rationally decide what is the right deal for you. Don't panic and buy the first thing you see, because most likely there will be the same item or a similar item coming up for auction in a few days.

Used Components

Although shopping for new components can be fun and rewarding, some of the best bargains in home theater are found by purchasing used components. Home theater continuously evolves, and the smart shopper can benefit from this trend. Some folks routinely replace their home theater components to ensure they are always on the cutting edge of technology. If you can find high-end used gear, you might be better served to look into buying it.

High-end models from the previous year often offer the same components, or better, than those found on the current year's budget models. For instance, component video switching was a common feature on high-end models but was not common on budget receivers in 2001. However, in 2002, many of the new budget home theater receivers featured component video switching ability (but cost more than a used high-end older model). High-end components also feature incredible craftsmanship and performance that are typically not rivaled by budget components.

Many websites are strictly devoted to buying and selling home theater gear. Use a search engine, such as Yahoo or Google, to find some of these sites. As with buying refurbished gear, you are taking a chance by dealing with an unknown party. Try to get as much information as possible from the seller before you send payment. If possible, try to use a payment service such as PayPal that allows you to pay via credit card. Buying components with your credit card allows you to maximize protection against unscrupulous sellers.

High-end audio gear, especially speakers, lasts for years. By letting someone else pay for the initial costs, you can then purchase the used items at a reduced rate. It's much the same as buying a used luxury car after it is several years old. Although the car isn't brand-new, it is likely to be higher quality than a brand-new budget car that you could buy for a little less money. Shop around until you find the used gear you're looking for, and always get a second opinion from a knowledgeable person about what the used gear should be worth.

CHAPTER 7

Things to Remember When Shopping

Regardless of where or from whom you choose to buy your components, there are things to remember when you begin your shopping quest. Shopping for home theater gear is typically time-intensive, so don't expect to finish up in a single day. The most important thing to do is to take your time, evaluate lots of components, and decide what sounds and looks best to you, not the salesperson. Be an informed consumer. Read product reviews, sales brochures, and message boards about the components that you want. There is a wealth of information waiting for you out there, so take advantage of it. Before you go into a store, read up on the hottest new products, but try to resist being overcome by marketing techniques.

Internet message boards are a good place to find out what most informed consumers think are the best products. Thousands of people keep up with home theater and love to share their opinions about products. I, for example, have helped thousands of people narrow down their shopping lists to the components that I feel best suit their budgets. Informed hobbyists tend to agree on a system for people looking to spend a certain amount of dollars. This gives you a good place to start, then you can add, modify, and delete from the list to custom-suit your needs.

When auditioning components, it helps to establish a frame of reference. If one shop shows you a scene from The Matrix and another retailer shows you a scene from Runaway Bride, chances are the system you watched The Matrix on will seem more impressive. To fairly evaluate a system, however, try to minimize external factors that influence your experience. If possible, have the salesperson show you a scene you are familiar with and saw elsewhere on a different system.

If you are testing speakers, have the salesperson set the system only to play through the speakers you are evaluating. If you are testing front speakers, have the salesperson turn off the subwoofer so you know the bass you are hearing is coming solely from the main speakers and not the expensive powered subwoofer. A speaker's ability to reproduce low frequencies can be masked greatly by a powered subwoofer.

Another helpful tip is to try to find a scene from a movie or a song that can isolate certain speakers or frequencies. If you need rear surround speakers, find a scene that showcases the rear speakers. I recommend a THX trailer on THX-certified DVD discs, such as Star Wars Episode I. It won't do you much good to go listen to rear surround speakers if the scene audition doesn't use the rear speakers well. Just remember that this is your system, so buy what sounds best to your ears.

8

Connecting All the Components

Connecting the various home theater components can tire and frustrate even the most devoted home theater user. Although it might seem you need a degree in electrical engineering to get all your devices to work together, if you understand each component's role, its inputs, and outputs, the job becomes manageable.

Most of us are much too excited to calmly follow directions provided with each device. Instead, we haphazardly rush through the setup until we have baffled ourselves—and then we opt for the instructions. Investing a small amount of time up front creating a wiring diagram saves you lots of time (no getting confused or doing and redoing the same things over and over again) and money (eliminates the risk of buying duplicate cables). Your wiring diagram should depict the wire, or series of wires, that will go in and out of each device. This proves especially important when you are working with the receiver and its multiple inputs.

After your system is properly wired, you face the daunting task of getting all your components to work (together). A home theater system does you no good if you can't figure out how to play a DVD.

This chapter guides you through connecting all your components, including identifying your connections, determining the cables you should use, and figuring out which of your remotes works best for your system.

Cables

Although the primary home theater components (receiver, DVD player, VCR, television, etc.) do all your major home theater work, cables are the essential links that convey sites and sounds between the components. Cables have many different shapes, sizes, lengths, and connection types. Coaxial, composite, component, and S-Video are the four standard cables you need to get your devices hooked up properly, but you also need to determine whether you should use analog and digital cables. In addition, you need to decide which type of speaker wire to use. Please don't forget to "round up" when buying cables. For instance, if you measure the desired length for one cable as 4.5 feet, you should buy one size larger than 4.5 feet, which, in this case, is likely to be 6 feet.

Video Cables

Understanding the different types of video cables and knowing advantages and disadvantages of each helps you determine which type of video connections to use. Chances are, your home theater needs at least two of the four following types of video connections. The cable should have its grade printed on it.

Coaxial Cables

Coaxial cables are the most basic and common cables in use today. Coaxial cables are a great, cost-effective way to distribute a signal over a long distance. (See Figure 8.1.) If you subscribe to a local cable television service, for instance, your television likely uses a coaxial cable to receive audio and video input. Even if you are using a cable box or satellite decoder, the signal probably comes into your house via a coaxial cable.

Figure 8.1
Coaxial cables are a cost-effective way to distribute a signal over a long distance

There are many types and grades of coaxial cables, but don't be fooled by the similar looks, as some cables are substantially better than others. Two common coaxial cable grades are RG-59 and RG-6. Although an RG-59 coaxial cable looks incredibly similar to an RG-6, the RG-6 is actually a much better cable. RG-6 cables typically feature increased shielding that enables them to transfer a signal with less degradation. This shielding also helps minimize outside interference from other electrically-powered sources. Even though RG-6 cables cost more than RG-59 cables (75 feet of RG-6 is about $20, whereas 75 feet of RG-59 is about $12), the increased picture quality makes them worth the money. If you have a digital satellite system, such as DirecTV or Dish Network, most likely the cable running from the satellite dish to your satellite receiver is an RG-6 grade coaxial cable.

Composite Cables

Most likely, you are already familiar with composite cables, the standard red-, yellow-, and white-tipped cables that come with almost every VCR, DVD, and TV. Composite cables use a standard RCA connection. These cables are capable of carrying video and audio, but the picture quality tends to be poor, because there's only one video cable and the video signal is completely transmitted via a single cable. In addition, although the yellow connector is often deemed the "video" cable, it has no different construction than the other cables; all three cables are identical. The coloring is simply to ensure you get the right inputs connected to the right outputs.

Composite cables are very common—and are therefore quite inexpensive. They convey an analog, or nondigital, signal between two devices and are commonly used to connect audio from a VCR, satellite receiver, or television into your receiver. Although you can find basic composite cables at really affordable prices, the signal quality may be less than satisfactory. See Figure 8.2. As a general rule, try not to use the cables provided with your equipment, as such cables are typically poor in quality.

Figure 8.2
Composite cables are the cheapest cables, but offer the worst signal quality

S-Video Cables

An S-Video cable only carries a video signal. Although more expensive than composite cables, S-Video cables offer a significantly better picture quality—enough to justify the cost. See Figure 8.3.

Figure 8.3
S-Video cables offer better picture quality than composite cables

Like composite cables, S-Video cables use a single cable to transfer the entire video signal. However, the similarities between the two cables end there. Composite cables carry all three colors (red, green, and blue) and brightness (whites and blacks) in a single video signal in one cable. S-Video divides the brightness and colors into separate signals within the same cable. By separating the brightness signals from the color signals, S-Video cables minimize color bleeding and help increase clarity and sharpness. Thus, you get a better picture.

Some older devices, such as VCRs, may not offer S-Video connections. In this case, you have to use composite connections. Remember, when shopping for a receiver, you should select a receiver that can handle S-Video switching.

As mentioned, S-Video only transmits a video signal. To obtain sound, you need to incorporate either a pair of composite cables or a digital audio cable. For instance, if you connect a DVD player to your television via an S-Video cable, you use a single S-Video cable for the video and a digital audio cable (either coaxial or optical) from the DVD player to the receiver for the audio. Figure 8.4 shows an example of this configuration.

Figure 8.4
S-Video cables are an affordable way to transfer a high-quality video signal

It is well-established that an S-Video cable transfers a better signal than a composite cable. This is because most picture sources today (DVD, satellite) actually store and process the picture as separate brightness and color signals. Using a composite cable requires that the source combine the signals and force the television to split it back out again to be sent to the set's driver and color decoder. Will you actually notice the difference? That depends. If you have a 27-inch or larger television set, the answer is yes, but if you have a small television, you probably won't notice the difference. So, should you spend the extra money for an S-Video cable? Well, a decent 6-foot composite cable costs about $15, whereas an S-Video cable of the same length costs approximately $20. In most situations, the improvement in picture quality is worth the extra five dollars.

Component Cables

DVD players introduced consumers to incredible digital surround sound. But incredible sound is only half of the equation, because without incredible visuals to complement the sound, the home theater experience is not the same. Most DVD players feature a new connection type, the component video connection. Component video is more expensive than S-Video, but it delivers the ultimate in picture quality.

Component video cables look very similar to composite video cables (see Figure 8.5). Consisting of three independent-but-bundled cables, component cables feature standard RCA type connectors (just like composite cables, but they also have heavier shielding to ensure maximum signal quality).

Figure 8.5
Component video
cables look similar
to composite cables
but deliver superior
image quality

Recall that S-Video divides the video signal into color and brightness signals. Component video goes another step by separating the color components into two separate signals; the increased signal separation leads to better color saturation and picture quality.

Many people wonder if they can use composite cables to transfer a component video signal. Does this work? The short answer is yes. The long answer is that component video cables feature increased shielding and a true 75-ohm resistance rating, which, in theory, means they transmit a better picture. Cable manufacturers and enthusiasts argue that a "true" component cable is the only way to go, but I think a quality composite cable suffices.

Component video connections offer added advantages beyond a better picture, though. Progressive scan signals can only be sent via component video connections. If your DVD player and television monitor support progressive scan, you definitely want to use those connections to obtain the 480p image that offers an even more impressive video image.

A DVD player's component video connections are typically marked as Y, Cb, and Cr. These are technical descriptions of the signal separations. Often, these connections are colored as red, green, and blue. HDTV-ready monitors also use component video connections to transfer high-definition signals from a decoder box to the monitor. Because HDTV has an even higher picture resolution than the progressive scan DVD format, it is often marked as Y, Pb, and Pr. The cable marked with Y carries the signal's luminance information. The Pb and Pr cables carry color difference information that is mathematically calculated. You should note that RGB and component video connections aren't the same. An RGB signal is a signal that has been split into the three primary colors (red, green, and blue). Because of the difference in the signals, RGB and component connections are not natively compatible. However, there are adapters that will convert an RGB signal to a component signal and vice versa.

DVD players and HDTV are the two highest quality picture sources available for home theater. It is no coincidence that both perform best with component video connections—they are that good. The big drawback, though, is that component video cables can be expensive, costing about $50 for a six-foot cable. Also, if you are striving for the ultimate in video quality, make sure you have a television that incorporates component video connections. However, if you are looking to free up some needed budget, S-Video signals are very comparable to component video signals on televisions that have a 36 inch or less diagonal length. If your television and DVD player both feature progressive scan ability, you should use component video connections to take advantage of the improvement that progressive scan makes.

Audio Cables

There are many different types of audio cables. Your setup most likely requires at least two types of audio cables, and the following section helps you identify which types of cables you may need.

Analog Stereo Cables

The most basic form of audio cable in home theater systems is a pair of stereo cables. (See Figure 8.6.) These cables are the red and white cables that often accompany the yellow cable in a composite video cable bundle. The red and white cables send an analog stereo signal between a device and a home theater receiver. As mentioned previously, the color coding on the connections is simply to ensure you get the right output connected with the corresponding input.

Analog stereo cables are usually affordable; you can find good cables for under $20. Try to find cables that feature good shielding, true 75-ohm resistance, and gold plated connections.

Figure 8.6
Analog stereo cables provide audio from nondigital devices, such as a VCR, to your home theater receiver

If you are running a composite video cable from a device, it makes sense to use a typical composite cable that has the video, left audio, and right audio cables bundled together. However, if you are planning to run S-Video from a source, you should buy a pair of analog stereo interconnects that only feature two cables bundled together. This helps minimize confusion when trying to organize your wiring configuration.

Digital Audio Cables

Digital audio cables transmit digital bitstreams from an audio source, such as a DVD player, to your home theater receiver. The home theater receiver receives the signal, processes it, and reproduces it. Digital audio cables provide the best audio quality, but as always, they are also more expensive than standard analog audio cables. You can expect to pay about $20 for a six-foot digital optical cable, whereas a standard six-foot analog audio cable costs approximately $12. Digital audio is typically available from DVD players, CD players, and some satellite receivers. If a component offers a digital audio output, you should use it, as this provides a better sound than an analog connection.

Digital audio cables come in two types: digital coaxial and optical (optical cables are sometimes called toslink cables; see Figure 8.7). A digital coaxial cable looks like a typical composite cable, but instead of being a bundle of two or three wires, it is a single wire (see Figure 8.8). Although the two cables differ in appearance and connection type (see Figure 8.9), they perform the same function. Although audio purists certainly argue about which of the two digital cables delivers a better signal, there is virtually no qualitative difference between them.

Figure 8.7
An optical cable transfers a digital signal from a source to the home theater receiver for processing

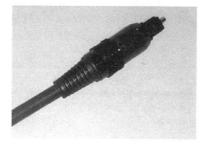

Figure 8.8
Digital coaxial cables are one of two options for getting a digital bitstream to your receiver

Figure 8.9
Digital coaxial and digital optical cables feature very different connection types

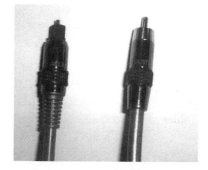

CHAPTER 8

Digital audio cables serve an important purpose in a home theater. They transmit the Dolby Digital, or DTS, bitstream from the DVD player to the home theater receiver. The home theater receiver, creating the amazing home theater sound, then processes this digital bitstream into surround sound.

Just like component cables, digital audio cables look remarkably similar to the plain, composite cables that come with your DVD player. Again, a typical composite cable can function as a digital coaxial cable; however, unless you buy a high-quality composite cable, the results may suffer. Although I recommend purchasing a digital coaxial cable, in a pinch, you can make do with a typical composite cable. Digital coaxial cables feature 75-ohm connections and quality shielding to ensure that no unwanted artifacts arrive in your digital signal. Brands don't seem to vary much in quality, but I have had good luck with Radio Shack's Gold series and Acoustic Research cables. Both brands are reasonably priced and superior to those included with your components.

Most home theater receivers feature more optical digital inputs than coaxial inputs. Most new DVD players feature both types of connections, but some only feature optical digital outputs. If your DVD player offers digital coaxial output, you may want to use the coaxial output and save the optical inputs on your receiver for devices only offering optical output.

Digital cables are essential in the setup of your home theater. To get Dolby Digital or DTS surround sound, you have to use one of the two types of digital connections. In most cases, you only need to use a digital connection from your DVD player to your receiver. Analog connections are also usually provided, but even with discs not encoded in Dolby Digital, most DVD players output the signal via the digital output, making a repetitive analog connection unnecessary.

Speaker Cable

The last link in your home theater system is the connection from your home theater receiver to your speakers. Each speaker in your system has two wires running from it to the receiver.

Before we delve into specifics in this section, I want to point out that speaker wire is a highly debated topic among home theater enthusiasts. Some believe that only the most expensive wire will do, paying hundreds of dollars for each speaker cable in their system. Others vouch that all wire is the same and run the cheapest cable they can find at their local hardware store.

This section helps identify which type of wire you should purchase for your home theater system and also the wire size you should run to each speaker. Then, we answer common questions about selecting the right length of speaker wire.

The first thing to understand about speaker wire is the different sizes available. Typical speaker wire used in home theater systems include 12-gauge, 16-gauge, and 20-gauge. The smaller the gauge, the larger the actual wire that conducts the signal. For instance, 12-gauge speaker wire has a larger diameter than a 20-gauge wire. See Figure 8.10.

Figure 8.10
Speaker wire is measured in gauges— the smaller the gauge, the larger the wire; shown here is 12-gauge wire

So, what gauge should you buy? That depends on how long each wire must run. A 12-gauge wire does a better job of conducting a signal over a long distance (twenty-five feet or more) than a 20-gauge, so if you are going to be running 30-foot wires, you should consider buying 12-gauge wire. For most budget theater systems, 12-gauge is probably the largest size of speaker wire you will need to run.

The smaller gauge wire is also more expensive than its fatter counterparts. The good news is that speaker wire in general is inexpensive and commonly priced by the foot. You can expect to pay about thirty to forty cents per foot for speaker wire. You get an even better rate (around twenty-five cents per foot in bulk) if you buy a spool of 50 or 100 feet. After you decide what size of speaker wire to use, you must determine how many total feet you need. Remember, you have to run speaker wire from your receiver to all five satellite speakers in your home theater system, including the surround channels. Another important thing to keep in mind is that you'll want to hide the wires to your rear surround channels, which typically requires running them around the edge of the room, through the walls, or under the carpet.

When buying speaker wire, you want to ensure that you buy the appropriate length. When deciding what cable length to use, use this handy tip: Run a string along the path between the two devices, and then measure the string. This gives you a good estimate of how long the cable needs to be. Don't forget to run the string all the way to the point of attachment to the speaker, including through the stands or up the wall. Often, people run the string to the point on the floor where the speaker is, but fail to account for the added vertical distance for the speaker cable to run through the speaker stand to the speaker. After you determine how many total feet you need for all speakers, add about 10 feet to that number. This gives you an extra two feet for each speaker cable run. It is always good to have a little extra; nobody can stretch a nine-foot cable into a ten-foot cable.

Another common question about speaker wire is "Do all the wires to my front three speakers need to be the same length?" Although I've never been able to discern a difference when using different length speaker wires, it is recommended to run equal length speaker wires for your front left, front center, and front right speakers. This ensures equal signal delay time across the front speakers.

Because speaker wire is relatively inexpensive when compared with the other cables in your home theater system, I suggest running 12-gauge speaker wire for all five speakers in your system. Although this size wire might seem too wide for the front three speakers, it is better to be safe than sorry. Many connectors are made with 12-gauge wire in mind, so it should provide good signal distribution to your rear speakers. Acoustic Research makes good quality, inexpensive speaker wire. I also buy speaker wire from home improvements stores, such as Home Depot or Lowe's, where they'll cut the wire to your precise measurements.

Regardless of where you buy your wire or what brand you buy, you should consider what type of termination you want to use for the wire ends. I prefer bare wire connections on my speakers. However, the copper in the bare wire quickly corrodes when exposed to oxygen, which can cause static in audio reproduction. To prevent this corrosion, you can "tin" your speaker wire ends. Tinning is the process of using a soldering gun to coat the copper wire with solder. Solder is resistant to corrosion and since the solder is relatively soft, the binding posts can make a good solid connection with the tinned wire end.

Making the Connections

You've done your research. You've purchased the right components. Now, it is time to link each part of your system so all parts work together. A small amount of time invested up front in proper wiring results in increased enjoyment with minimal stress. The following section guides you through the process of wiring your system. We help you develop a wiring diagram that lets you know the exact cables you need.

Creating a Wiring Diagram

A wiring diagram is a simple sketch that shows how the various components of a home theater system connect to each other. Of course, this sample wiring diagram is for a typical budget home theater; the particulars of your system may vary.

Your home theater should contain the following components:

- Television
- DVD player
- Home theater receiver
- VCR
- Satellite receiver
- Five-speaker surround sound system
- Powered subwoofer

When creating a wiring diagram, you should first identify what each component does and if that component will receive an input, send an output, or both. For instance, a DVD player typically only sends an output signal, both audio and video, to another source. However, a home theater receiver receives signals from components like a DVD player but also sends signals to the television and to the speakers.

In the previous hypothetical system, the television is strictly an input device. Its sole function is to receive the video signal sent from the receiver, which handles the audio that accompanies the video. This means that we only need a video cable for the television. This cable travels from the video output of the home theater receiver to an input on the television.

So, which type of video cable should you choose? That depends on what video you have in your system. If your television monitor handles component video, a component video cable works best. Most budget home theater receivers only incorporate S-Video switching, though. To use component video outputs with these receivers, you need to run the video output from the source component, like the DVD player, to the television. This is common. By running the cable straight to the television, you minimize the number of connections and processing that occurs on the video signal.

Most likely, the system you build will need to use both S-Video and composite connections. As mentioned, most budget home theater receivers don't handle component video switching, so to use component video, you must run the output from the source straight to the television. Then, to incorporate your S-Video connections, you must run all the S-Video sources into the receiver and allow it to handle the video switching for you.

If you have a device that features only composite video output, your wiring diagram will be a little more complicated. Most receivers don't convert a composite video signal into an S-Video signal. This means you need to run your composite sources directly into your television set. This shouldn't be a huge issue as most devices offer at least S-Video outputs. However, if you are using an older VCR, you may find it only has composite video outputs. If this is the case, you should use composite video connections to hook up the VCR to the receiver. If your receiver doesn't feature a composite video output, then you must run a coaxial cable from the VCR to the television.

The next device in our system is the DVD player. The DVD player is responsible for sending an audio and video signal to the home theater receiver and possibly the television. Because the DVD player doesn't accept a signal from any other device, you can see that it is clearly an output-only device. Therefore, in the wiring diagram, there is a video output and an audio output (see Figure 8.11). You have to decide which type of video output to use, but for now, you can simply label the wires "Video Output" and "Audio Output." If you have a television monitor that is at least 36 inches in diagonal length and a DVD player that has component video capabilities, I highly recommend using a component video connection (if not, use S-Video).

Figure 8.11
A diagram showing the wiring required for a DVD player

DVD

Component Video Output

Digital Optical Output

Now, let's make wiring decisions about the VCR. (See Figure 8.12.) Because you probably already own a VCR, this part of the wiring diagram should be straightforward. If you plan on using your VCR to record television shows, it acts as both an input and an output device. The VCR receives an input signal, most likely using a coaxial cable from a cable jack in the wall, and it also outputs a signal to the television monitor so you can view the material being played. If your VCR features S-Video, I recommend that you use an S-Video connection (if the best connection type available is composite, then use that connection). Your wiring diagram should show the input, which requires probably both audio and video in a single coaxial cable, and the output cable, which is most likely separated into audio and video signals carried in composite cables.

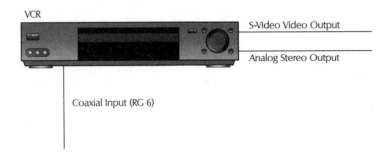

Figure 8.12
The wiring diagram for a VCR depicts both an input and an output (this VCR offers you the option of using either an S-Video output or an analog stereo output)

An increasingly common device in most homes is a digital satellite receiver, such as those by DirecTV and Dish Network. These satellite receivers have wiring characteristics similar to a VCR, relying on an input signal from a coaxial cable and an output cable with separate audio and video. Most satellite receivers feature S-Video and composite outputs, but few feature component video outputs. Just like in the VCR diagram, the satellite receiver should show a single input and two outputs (one for video and one for audio), as shown in Figure 8.13. Some satellite receivers can send the digital audio bitstream to the receiver. If your receiver has an optical or digital coaxial connection, be sure to use that connection. A digital connection to your receiver creates better sound reproduction. An added benefit of using digital audio connections is that you get Dolby Digital programming. Many pay-per-view movies and some premium movie channels, such as HBO, broadcast with Dolby Digital audio.

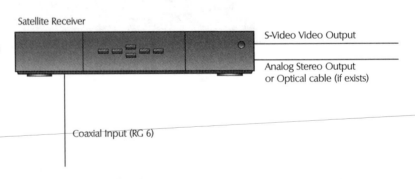

Figure 8.13
Digital satellite receivers have one input and two outputs (one for audio and one for video)

At this point, you've created a good portion of your wiring diagrams. However, you may be wondering where all these outputs from source components are going. Now that you have the hang of creating wiring diagrams, let's tackle how to integrate the home theater receiver into the diagram. The home theater receiver is the most complicated device to wire, as it has many inputs and an output. The receiver gets audio, and sometimes video, signals from the DVD player. It can also receive a signal from the VCR, the satellite receiver, and the personal television recorder. The receiver takes in all these signals and selects which source will be output to the speakers and television monitor. It outputs a video signal to the television monitor and sends an audio signal to each of the speakers in the surround sound speaker system.

You first want to get the DVD player signal input into the receiver properly. If you're using component video connections, you want to connect the video output of the DVD player to the component video inputs on your television. If you're using your receiver's S-Video switching ability, then let your wiring diagram reflect that by drawing the video output from the DVD player to an input on the receiver. For the audio portion, you should show the digital audio output, either coaxial or optical, from the DVD player to a digital input on the receiver. See Figure 8.14 for an example of how this configuration should look.

Figure 8.14
The DVD player sends an audio, and possibly a video, signal to the home theater receiver

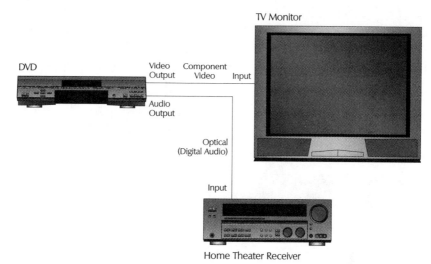

The VCR and satellite receivers connect to the home theater receiver in a similar fashion as the DVD player does. If you're using the receiver to pass the video signal from the VCR to the television, be sure that your diagram depicts this. If not, simply show the audio portion going into the receiver and the video portion connecting to the television monitor.

In Figure 8.15, you can see a sample of how the diagram should look after all the inputs have been directed into the home theater receiver. In our example, I have the receiver doing the video switching for the VCR and satellite receiver but not the DVD player. Of course, this assumes that all these devices have S-Video outputs, and that you've chosen to use this connection method. Your diagram will look slightly different if you choose to use S-Video cables to connect the video signal from your DVD player to your receiver.

Figure 8.15
The home theater receiver is a central hub for various signals coming and going from your components

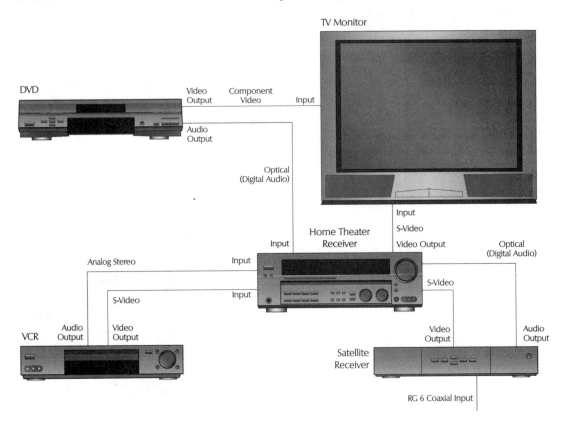

As you can see in Figure 8.15, many devices run into the home theater receiver but none goes out. The outputs are not to be overlooked and this section details what output connections need to be made. Besides having to deliver a video signal to the television monitor (unless you are running the video signals directly to your television monitor), the receiver needs to send the audio signals to each speaker in the surround sound system. Each of the speakers requires a speaker cable consisting of a positive and negative cable, but the two cables will be connected and are essentially a single cable. The powered subwoofer needs a low-level connection, commonly known as a composite cable.

DEPICTING SPEAKER WIRES

In your wiring diagram, be sure each speaker wire runs from the home theater receiver to an individual speaker. This becomes important later when we start incorporating the cable lengths into our diagram.

At this point, your diagram should be near completion. It should show the inputs to the receiver, the outputs from the receiver, and the input into the television monitor. Also, it should show the speaker wires running to each speaker. The powered subwoofer cable is actually a composite cable carrying a low-level signal to the subwoofer's amplifier. Your diagram should resemble Figure 8.16.

Figure 8.16
The wiring diagram is near completion, showing all the wires and cables necessary to hook up the surround sound system

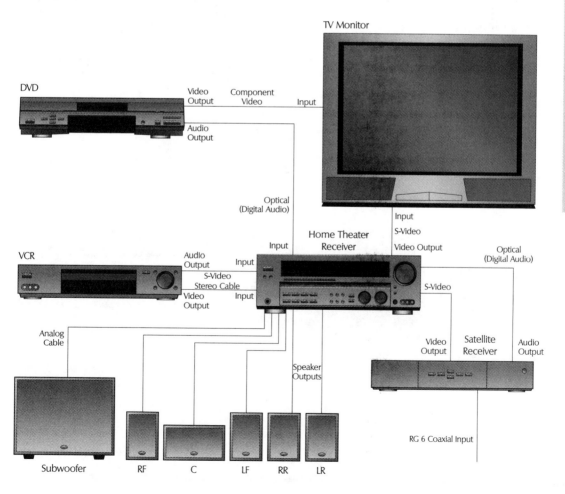

The last step to completing the wiring diagram is to determine how long each cable should be. First, take your measurements for each cable, and then write each cable's length down on your wiring diagram next to that particular cable. This allows you to have a single sheet of paper that tells you what size and type of wire or cable you need for each connection, allowing ease in purchasing. See Figure 8.17.

Figure 8.17
Write the length of each wire in your wiring diagram to make cable buying simple

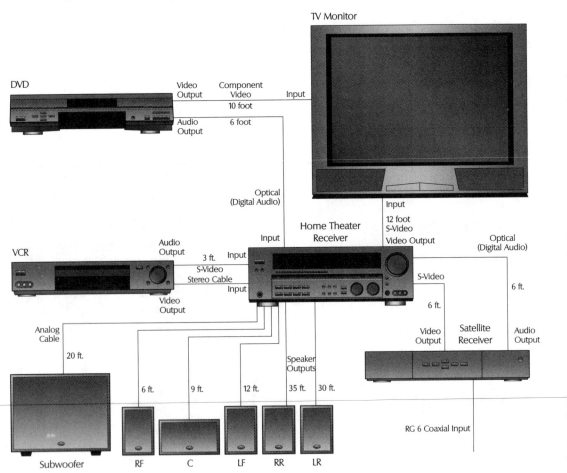

ALLOW FOR MOVEMENT

When measuring speaker wire lengths, be sure to add at least an extra foot to each speaker's wire in case you need to alter the speaker's placement. The next chapter shows you how to optimize your sound by properly positioning your speakers and calibrating the audio and video portions of your home theater system.

Hooking Up Each Device

You've created a wiring diagram. You've bought your cables. Now comes the time to take the cables you've purchased and physically create the connections between components. These connections should be relatively simple to make because the wiring diagram shows exactly where each cable goes.

Connecting the DVD Player

Remember that DVD players only have outputs. However, most DVD players feature composite, S-Video, and component video outputs as well as coaxial and optical digital audio outputs. You should have already decided what type of connection you are using, so look for that connection type on the rear of the DVD player. Most DVD players have a label on each output. If the outputs are not labeled, examine the instruction manual for your DVD player to determine which connection types are available. If you've chosen to use an optical digital audio cable, there is most likely a dust cap on the output for that cable. If your DVD player is plugged into a power source and you don't see a red light in the optical digital output, the dust cap is probably still in place. If so, remove the dust cap by pulling it out, and store it in a safe place. When not using the optical connection, the dust cap should be on.

After identifying which type of connection to use, simply connect the cables. When laying out the cables, make every attempt to keep the cables that carry audio and video signals separated from the power cords, to avoid interference. If you must cross the power cords, try to cross the signal cables and the power cables at a 90-degree angle, and always avoid running the cables parallel to the power cords.

Connecting the VCR

As we described earlier, the VCR has inputs and outputs. Most likely, you need to run a coaxial cable from a cable jack in the wall to the VCR for an input signal. However, if you are using a satellite receiver, you need to run composite or S-Video cables from the satellite receiver to the corresponding input for the type of connection that you are running. You may also need to initialize your VCR to the composite cable inputs before it will work properly. This step tells your VCR to look for an input from the composite connections instead of the coaxial connection. See the documentation that came with your VCR to determine what must be done to set your VCR to accept an input.

Connecting the Receiver

Due to the number of incoming signals, the receiver is the most labor-intensive component to set up. However, the wiring diagram should help identify where each incoming signal should go. It is good practice to wire each component individually, and check the connection before moving onto another component. After the components are wired and configured, the speaker wires need to be connected from the receiver to the speakers.

The first order of business is to connect the DVD player. If you are running the video signal from the DVD player to the receiver, run that cable first. Most receivers label for each input, but if your receiver doesn't have labels on the inputs, you should consult the instruction manual for the home theater receiver. For example, you may see "DVD" and "VCR" inputs. It is wise to use the corresponding input for each device for ease and simplicity.

Component, composite, and digital coaxial cables attach easily. Simply push the male end of the cable into the corresponding female input. Be sure that you connect corresponding colors on the input and output, and also make sure that you go from an output to an input.

S-Video connections are very similar to other connection types, but due to the pin layout, you must be careful to insert the cable properly (it's the unusual pin layout that requires extra attention). Make note of the top of the cable and try not to rotate the cable as you begin to make the connection. If the cable is not lined up properly, you run the risk of bending one of the connection pins. See Figure 8.18.

FIGURE 8.18

Take extra care not to bend a connection pin when inserting an S-Video cable

Digital connections require a little extra setup. Although making the physical connection is simple, you must first assign the digital input to a specific input on the receiver, because digital connections are not tied to a single input. Go into your receiver's setup to assign the digital input. Pressing a 'Setup or Menu' button on the home theater receiver's remote control typically does this. Each receiver differs in the process of assigning the input, so ensure that you read your receiver's instructions.

The easiest digital connection to set up and test comes from your DVD player. If you have your DVD player set up with a digital connection to your receiver, you can test it now. Make sure that you don't have any analog cables connecting your DVD player to your receiver. Turn on your DVD player and your receiver and begin playing a DVD. If your connection is set up properly, your receiver should indicate that it is receiving a digital signal and you should hear sound. If you don't hear sound, it is likely that you haven't assigned your digital input correctly.

The most critical connections run from the receiver to the speakers. Each of the five satellite speakers have positive and negative connections on the back panel of the receiver. There are a variety of speaker wire connectors to ease connections, including banana plugs, spades, and pins. Some of these connectors require the use of a soldering iron and some of them simply screw on to the bare wire. Banana plugs are the most common type of connection, and they do simplify connecting the wires to the receiver. However, banana plugs cost around $5 for a pair. As mentioned earlier, many folks simply "tin" the bare speaker wires with a soldering iron and use a bare wire connection. (See Figure 8.19.) The bare wire connection is the least expensive way to connect your speakers, but be aware that the wires can oxidize over time and diminish your system's sound.

When connecting speaker wires, ensure that the connection is solid, because loose wires can cause grounding problems. Grounding is when part of the speaker wire touches metal instead of the speaker terminal. Grounding causes your speakers to pop from the electrical signal grounding itself to the metal. Also, remember to periodically check your connections, because speaker wires tend to compress and thus their connections might become loose. If using banana plugs, ensure that a good solid connection is made when inserting the plug into the speaker binding post. Banana plugs plug directly into the binding post on the receiver, much like a composite cable plugs into an input. If using bare wire or pins, unscrew the binding post and slip the wire or pin through the drilled hole in the binding post, and then tighten the binding post.

FIGURE 8.19

Speaker connections are vital; shown here are a "bare wire" speaker connection (left) and a connection using high-quality banana plugs (right)

CHAPTER 8

Speakers have a positive and a negative terminal. When connecting the wires, first connect the negative speaker terminal on the receiver to the negative speaker terminal on the speaker. Some speaker wires are marked, but some aren't. If the speaker wires you are using are not marked, you must trace the wire from one terminal to the other to ensure the speakers are connected properly. Chapter 9 addresses how to test your speakers.

Connecting the Satellite Receiver

The satellite receiver connects to the home theater receiver similarly to the DVD player. You need to run a video cable, most likely via an S-Video cable, and an audio cable. Many digital satellite receivers offer a digital audio output to allow digital audio to be routed directly to a home theater receiver. If your satellite receiver offers a digital audio connection, try to use it. Many pay-per-view movies on digital satellite systems offer Dolby Digital audio, but you can only take advantage of Dolby Digital if you have the receiver connected via a digital audio connection.

There are a few digital satellite receivers that feature component video outputs. If you have such a receiver, I recommend using these outputs. Digital satellite systems can offer good picture quality, and component video connections allow you to obtain the optimal picture from your satellite receiver.

Controlling the System

Every component in your system probably has its own remote control. Unless you want to have a pile of remote controls, you should consolidate the functionality. Many remotes included with home theater receivers have preprogrammed codes that allow them to control other devices, such as television monitors and VCRs. Some receiver remotes even feature learning ability. This learning ability allows the remote to listen to another remote, copy the signal, and reproduce the signal.

Depending on which receiver and remote you have, you may also want to consider investing in a universal remote control. Universal remotes often feature increased memory that allows them to learn more codes from other remote controls. Universal remotes also have the ability to create and run macros, a series of commands programmed into a single button click.

If possible, use as many preprogrammed codes as you can. These codes are already stored in the remote control's memory and therefore don't take up any memory that can otherwise be used for learning codes. With a limited amount of internal memory built into the remote control, don't expect to learn every button from each remote. To keep costs down, most universal remote controls come with a small amount of internal memory storage to store infrared codes. When setting up your remote control, try to minimize the number of buttons you need to memorize. Keep the other remotes nearby but out of site, in case you need them.

Keep in mind that the receiver can control the audio and video switching. Therefore, the receiver's remote natively knows how to switch between components. It also natively knows how to control the volume. However, you need to be able to control things, such as the Play and Stop buttons on your DVD player. You may also want to think about creating a macro button that powers on or powers off all of your components to make your system easier to use.

An example of a competent remote that accompanies a receiver is the remote that comes with the Onkyo TX-DS595. This remote features learning ability, the ability to perform macros, and thousands of preprogrammed codes. It can store 8 macros, each of which can contain up to 16 commands. And it allegedly can learn up to 408 commands from other remotes.

If you have decided the receiver's remote is not going to be able to handle your system well enough, find a universal remote to do the job. If you are looking for a budget remote, I suggest giving serious consideration to the 15-2104 remote made by Radio Shack, as seen in Figure 8.20. Radio Shack remotes are very similar to the all-in-one remotes that you see in large electronics stores.

FIGURE 8.20

A good universal remote with learning capability, such as the Radio Shack 15-2104, helps you manage your home theater system

If you want to invest in an incredible but pricey remote control, consider the Philip's Pronto. This LCD remote features an almost endless number of possibilities, but programming it also requires a more technical background than an all-in-one or Radio Shack remote control. This LCD remote connects to your home computer and allows you to create custom layouts and program device codes. The downside to the LCD is its high price tag—it's well over $200. However, if you have a complex system and want the ultimate in flexibility, the Pronto is tough to beat.

Now that your system is hooked up and you've been able to eliminate all those unnecessary remotes, the next chapter shows you how to make sure you get the most out of your system.

CHAPTER 8

9

Getting the Most Out of Your Home Theater

Every home theater enthusiast wants an outstanding home theater experience. However, maximizing that experience requires preparation, calibration, and experimentation. You must prepare your environment—your home theater room—for optimal viewing and listening. You must calibrate your system's audio and video settings. And, you must experiment with your overall setup—from testing speaker placement to analyzing lighting nuances—to see what works best. This chapter walks you through these steps, offering tips, tricks, and techniques for getting the most out of your home theater.

Optimal Home Theater Environments

Thanks to its shape, size, and furnishings, every home theater room has physical peculiarities that give it a unique layout, look, and feel, all of which contribute to its overall acoustical signature. A square room with carpeted floors, for instance, has a very different effect on the sound emanating from your system than a rectangular room with high ceilings and hardwood floors. A room with square proportions sounds different than a rectangular room, even when using the same equipment. Often, rooms with unconventional shapes and geometry, such as cathedral ceilings and open sides, lead to the best sound. Square rooms have a tendency to reflect sounds, causing unwanted noise from the reflections. Furnishings in the room can also help to minimize the amount of sound reflections.

The type of flooring in your room can also affect the performance of your speakers. Hardwood floors reflect signals much more than carpeted areas and can negatively affect the sound by reflecting sounds and causing unwanted reverberation. If you have carpet, try to use carpet spikes. These spikes help make contact with the concrete slab under the carpet and help to eliminate vibrations. If you have hardwood flooring, these spikes can damage your floor, so be sure to set a solid object, such as a penny, under the spikes.

Unless you have the luxury of building a dedicated home theater room, you'll likely have to work with a preexisting room. The goal in this situation is to make the best of what you have to work with. If your theater room has hardwood floors, you should consider using area rugs or oversized couches to help minimize sound wave reflections. If your room has open doorways on one side, you will likely need to calibrate your system to ensure that both left and right side speakers are producing the same overall volume levels. Regardless of your room's acoustical signature, your system will benefit from a thorough calibration.

Calibrating Your Home Theater System

Although it usually isn't feasible to remodel your entire room to obtain better sound, it is quite possible to rearrange and adjust the settings on your existing components to optimize your current setup. That's where calibration—the process of positioning, adjusting, and tweaking your system to achieve maximum performance—comes in. You can calibrate your system by using a few simple tools and techniques discussed in the following sections, and you won't regret doing it, as you will enhance your system's sound and picture quality. After all, it doesn't make much sense to buy an expensive new television monitor and then not calibrate it. Often, a properly calibrated inexpensive television can look as good as or better than a more expensive uncalibrated monitor, because most television monitors come with extremely bright settings that are far from optimal.

Tools of the Trade

There are several tools that are handy to have in order to help calibrate your system. You don't need to spend a great deal of money on these tools, and they are available in a range of prices.

The Decibel Meter

Although your ears are the ultimate judges of how your system sounds, a decibel meter (see Figure 9.1) is invaluable for getting your system to operate optimally. A decibel meter measures the sound pressure level (SPL). The SPL is measured in decibels and allows you to accurately measure your volume. By knowing how loud a signal is being reproduced, you can set your system to re-create the sounds at the level they should be heard. Decibel meters also provide you a way to ensure that all your speakers produce equal amounts of volume at the listening position. A common and affordable decibel meter is the Radio Shack analog unit (Cat. #: 33-2050), which sells for under $40 and is well worth it. For simple home theater calibration, this analog unit works fine; there is no need to buy the more expensive digital unit. That said, I must point out that the Radio Shack digital unit (Cat #. 33-2055) has several more features than the analog unit, such as the ability to show average levels. However, the added features also add to the price of the digital model (it sells for about $50). In addition, it is easier to obtain an average reading using the analog version. The digital version displays the current audio output, but as you adjust volume, the output level reading fluctuates and can be hard to pinpoint.

Figure 9.1
A decibel meter is an essential tool in obtaining maximum performance from your home theater

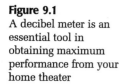

The Calibration Disc

A decibel meter is only one of the two essential tools used to get the best possible audio and video performance from your home theater calibration. The other is a calibration disc—a DVD disc with test patterns and diagnostics that help you optimize your system. Calibration discs include tests that help you adjust your video monitor's brightness, contrast, hue, tint, color, and flesh tone controls.

To properly calibrate the audio portion of your home theater, the decibel meter is used in combination with audio test signals played from the calibration disc. Calibration discs also come with color strips—small strips of tinted plastic that aid in setting color controls on your television monitor. These color strips are usually red, green, and blue. You look through the strip as the test pattern on your monitor is displayed. Then, you simply adjust the color and tint controls on your monitor to obtain the most accurate colors.

It wouldn't be a complete home theater calibration without test patterns to obtain the maximum sound. Many different test patterns help identify problems with phase, location, and frequency response. The most important feature of calibration discs, however, is the inclusion of test patterns that send a frequency to a single speaker, allowing you to measure and adjust the output level of that speaker. Although this asset might seem somewhat trivial, it is probably the most crucial home theater calibration. By evaluating and adjusting the output level of each speaker, you make sure that all your speakers produce the exact same volume level.

CHAPTER 9

Several calibration discs exist, and each has its advantages and disadvantages. The most commonly used calibration discs are Avia, Video Essentials, and Sound & Vision Home Theater Tune Up. Each helps guide you through tuning both your audio and video to help you obtain maximum results. Each disc also benefits from being used in conjunction with a decibel meter, which obtains accurate readings on sound level output. Although you can attempt to set sound level outputs by ear, you get much more accurate and consistent volume levels from your speakers by using a decibel meter.

Avia is the most thorough calibration disc (see Figure 9.2), but it is also the hardest disc to navigate—and one of the most expensive, costing around $40. Avia provides a tremendous number of audio and video test patterns and is the favorite of hard-core enthusiasts. That's because Avia focuses more on audio than video; its audio calibration chapters are second to none. The video calibration tests are adequate and they should suffice for the basic home theater user. Novice users might have trouble navigating test patterns and taking full advantage of the increased audio and video test patterns and features. If you are new to the calibration game and your budget is tight, you might consider buying one of the cheaper, easier-to-use calibration discs (covered in the following sections).

Figure 9.2
Avia is a favorite calibration disc for enthusiasts looking for maximum audio and video performance

Video Essentials is another advanced calibration DVD (see Figure 9.3). Like Avia, it features numerous audio and video test patterns. However Avia focuses more on audio, whereas Video Essentials has a reputation for helping you get the best picture out of your video monitor. Video Essentials is similar in price to Avia, usually running around $40 to $50, and is intuitively easier (more user-friendly) for the novice. Note: Video Essentials is currently being revised and redesigned, so it may be wise to wait for the new, improved version before buying this disc.

Figure 9.3
Video Essentials is a
great calibration disc for
video calibrations

A new entry on the calibration disc scene is Sound & Vision Home Theater Tune Up, a disc from
the magazine Sound & Vision. This is by far the most inexpensive calibration disc, with a price
tag under $20. Although not as advanced as the other two calibration discs, it has enough video
test patterns and audio test sounds for the average user. This disc features the basic calibration
essentials, but fails to offer the large quantity of patterns and signals available in the more costly
calibration discs. If you are looking for a basic, inexpensive calibration disc, though, the Sound
& Vision Home Theater Tune Up is probably a logical buy. See Figure 9.4.

Figure 9.4
Home Theater Tune Up
is a cost-effective
calibration disc that's
great for beginners

CHAPTER 9

A final option is cost-effective but basic. Some DVDs, such as Fight Club, have calibration tests included on the DVD. The calibrations on these discs are simple, but they do help bring your system settings closer to optimum level. Just bear in mind that these basic calibrations attached to content discs don't come close to offering the full-system calibration provided by the aforementioned calibration DVDs.

Performing the Calibrations

Regardless of which calibration disc you select, you use essentially the same techniques to get your system in top shape. You should calibrate your video first and then your audio. Let's step through the calibration process.

Calibrating Your Video Monitor

The settings on a new television are far from optimal, usually incredibly bright, creating a state that many enthusiasts call "torch mode." RPTVs are especially notorious for being horribly calibrated from the factory. Rear projection and CRT tube-based televisions both greatly benefit from proper brightness, contrast, and color settings. RPTVs also greatly benefit from basic alignment of the three color "guns." The basic process for calibrating the settings on television sets doesn't differ between display types, but rear projection sets require additional steps to ensure optimum picture quality. RPTVs use three "guns" (red, green, and blue) to project an image onto the screen. To obtain an optimal picture, these three color "guns" must be properly aligned at various points in the screen. If they're misaligned, you get a fuzzy, dull picture that will undoubtedly leave you dissatisfied.

Video monitor calibrations are critical. A poorly calibrated monitor doesn't just give you a poor picture; it may actually permanently burn your screen. With calibration, you can make your budget video monitor look and sound better than a more expensive system that has not been properly calibrated.

Many settings on your television set interact with each other. For instance, contrast and brightness both affect how dark the picture appears. Please keep in mind, too, that a properly calibrated video monitor looks dark at first, so give yourself time to adjust to it.

Adjusting the Brightness Level

Adjust the brightness setting first. Brightness is defined as the level of black in the picture. The lower the brightness setting, the more black in the picture; the higher the brightness setting, the more white (less black) in the picture. So, low brightness equals more black, which leads to an overall darker picture. Improper brightness settings can make black images appear navy blue or dark gray. The factory setting is typically high, meaning your picture will look bright before you start to calibrate it.

The amount of ambient light—light from windows and lighting fixtures—in the room affects the brightness setting. When attempting to calibrate the brightness setting, ensure the room has a typical amount of ambient light. A typical amount is the amount of light you would have in the room as you normally watch television. If you typically watch television with the shades drawn and the lights off, then those are the room conditions you should use when performing video calibrations. Most people typically watch more television in the evening, when there is much less ambient light. In this case, you want to begin calibration procedures after the sun sets.

To best test the brightness, find a scene with high contrast. The test patterns on the calibration discs often use a very bright white against a black background. The optimum brightness setting allows black colors to appear black instead of gray. However, if you set the brightness too low, fine details are lost. Brightness settings vary on every television, but typical settings are usually a third of the maximum level. Brightness test patterns typically have a grayscale object on one side of the screen and two dark bars on the other side. One of the dark bars is absolute black, and the other is slightly lighter than absolute black. The proper brightness setting should allow you to see the lighter of the two dark bars but not the absolute black bar.

Be aware that as the average picture level (APL) changes, your set's ability to hold black levels may change. For instance, your television monitor will likely hold black levels very well on dark scenes but may have trouble holding black levels on bright scenes. With that in mind, make sure that you test your brightness setting on both a low-APL scene and a high-APL scene. The calibration discs provide both types of scenes to help you obtain the correct setting.

Adjusting the Contrast Level

Contrast is the level of white in the picture. A high contrast level makes a picture look washed out and the details on white objects nearly invisible. A low contrast level does the same for the dark objects. Contrast and brightness affect each other, so after you have obtained the proper contrast level, be sure to check that your brightness level is still in the correct setting.

The calibration discs often feature a screen that's half black and half white. On the side of the screen is a vertical line that is black in the white section of the screen and white in the black section. A contrast level that is too high makes the line bend, as the television monitor has trouble holding the white level.

If your set has a sharpness control, ensure that is turned off or is at its lowest possible setting before attempting to gain proper contrast level. When contrast levels are too high, blooming occurs. Blooming is a condition in which white areas in the picture begin to expand as the contrast is turned up. This is caused by your television monitor not being able to control the white level at that setting. The proper white level should be found before the point that blooming begins to occur.

Brightness and contrast settings affect each other. The calibration discs excel at helping you understand the settings and how they affect each other. Before jumping into getting the settings correct, it is a good idea to sit down and carefully watch and listen to the description of the test, what to look for, and observe as the disc simulates changing the setting. This gives you a better understanding of what you are trying to accomplish, and ultimately makes it easier for you to obtain the correct setting.

Adjusting the Color Settings

One of the most recognizable problems with a television set is incorrect color balance. Examples of an incorrect color balance are green grass that looks blue and a white face that's too red. Many television sets come from the factory set to display one color more predominantly than others. This tendency is often described as "push." Some Mitsubishi television sets, for instance, push red, meaning they display a picture that displays more red than blue or green.

Many calibration discs provide color strips to help you accurately set color balance. These color strips are red, green, and blue. The calibration disc displays a test pattern with a color, such as blue, and you use the corresponding color strip to obtain the correct setting. While looking through the color strip, adjust the setting until you cannot distinguish between the two colors on the screen.

Adjusting the Tint Settings

Just as brightness and contrast affect each other, color and tint settings interact. When the tint settings are too high or too low, the picture appears too red or too green. The proper setting should be in between these two points, where things look the most natural. Again, color strips help identify the optimal setting for tint.

Before you adjust your tint settings, turn off all automatic color settings (also called flesh tone controls). These settings can skew your overall settings and keep you from gaining the correct tint setting. Automatic color settings on most sets can be disabled in the television's menu. Also, if your television monitor includes color settings, such as "cool," "medium," and "warm," use the medium setting. This is usually the most neutral setting.

Although color settings control the amount of blue in the picture, tint controls the amount of green and red. If your tint setting is too high, you may see colors bleed onto neighboring colors. If this is the case, lower the setting to keep the colors from bleeding onto each other.

Adjusting Scan Velocity Modulation Settings

Scan Velocity Modulation, (SVM), is another setting that may adversely affect your rear projection set. SVM is present in CRT tube-based television sets and plasma displays, but it is more apparent on the larger screen sizes of rear projection television monitors. SVM is similar to sharpness settings, because it adds information to the picture to smooth transitions between colors. But this addition can actually reduce detail, which is why most home theater users prefer that SVM be disabled.

Disabling SVM is different on each television, so consult your television manual to determine if your set can disable SVM through a menu setting. For example, Toshiba rear projection televisions (RPTVs) can disable SVM by beginning adjustments in "Film" mode and saving preferences. To find more information about disabling SVM on your particular set, try consulting the Internet, as there are many sites with brand- and model-specific information about how to turn off SVM.

Adjusting Rear Projection Specific Settings

RPTVs are the choice for many home theater systems. Although RPTVs offer a significantly larger picture, if not properly configured, the picture can be less than satisfactory. RPTVs need to have the projection guns aligned properly to obtain a crisp picture. Alignment of the three guns is better and worse at various positions on the screen. Convergence is the alignment of the red, green, and blue guns. Most RPTVs offer some form of adjustment through the menus.

If you are an advanced user and want to extract the best picture from your RPTV, you can do a lot of tweaking. Many adjustments require the use of an advanced menu set, often referred to as "service" or "designer" mode. These advanced settings, such as a more-detailed convergence grid to align the color guns, are used by trained technicians to fix problems and gain improved picture quality. If you think this is something you want to try, the first step is to purchase a factory service manual. This service manual explains the advanced settings in detail. Service manual adjustments are the intermediate step between having basic video adjustments and having an ISF-certified technician perform a full-video calibration on your system.

Calibrating Your Audio System

Just like the video monitor, your audio system also needs to be calibrated properly. Subtle sounds may be lost if it's not. Because each room has its own acoustical fingerprint, sound calibration is necessary to ensure that you hear the soundtrack the way it was intended to be heard. Calibration DVDs, in conjunction with a decibel meter, give you a reference level to set each speaker's output level. Calibration enables you to ensure that all speakers in your system have the same output level when given the same signal. It also helps you identify if you have speaker placement problems and if your speakers are operating out of phase. Calibration also helps you identify and set up problems.

If you don't understand the point of audio calibration thoroughly, think of it like this: If you put the speaker setup from a rock concert in your living room, it doesn't take much volume to be overwhelming. Likewise, if you try to fill a concert hall with your home system, it would likely need an incredible amount of volume to be heard in the distant rows. These are examples of how a different system and a different room affect audio reproduction differently.

Positioning the Speakers

Positioning the speakers is most important when setting up the system. Although each room is different, there are some basic rules that you can apply to your system. Speaker placement should precede a full audio calibration. To obtain optimal sound, you need to position your speakers in the best position for sound reproduction in your room. After you have positioned your speakers properly, a full-audio calibration lets you know that all the speakers are reproducing equal sound and volume levels.

The center channel is the easiest speaker to place. In most systems, the center channel sits directly on top of the television monitor. However, there are some tips that can help you gain maximum performance from your center channel. For starters, your center channel should be aimed directly at the primary listening area. Often, the center channel is aimed above ear level. Don't do that. Consider elevating the rear of the speaker, so the speaker is aimed down at ear level. Conversely, if your speaker is positioned below your television, raise the front of the speaker to aim the speaker upwards.

AIMING SPEAKERS

A laser pointer can be a valuable tool when aiming speakers. By attaching a laser pointer to a speaker, you can easily see exactly where the speaker is being aimed.

The left and right speakers are the next speakers you should position. They work together with the center channel for Dolby Digital reproduction, but they also work independently when listening to two-channel stereo signals. To create proper stereo-imaging, the speakers should be at least six feet apart, but try to keep them within ten to eleven feet of each other. In addition, the speakers should be placed against the same wall if possible and should be equidistant from the center channel.

Optimally, the left and right speakers should be slightly in front of the television monitor. This is to account for the increased distance to the listening area. The best speaker positioning creates a phantom image between the left and right speakers that sounds as if a center channel is in use. If the speakers are too far apart, you may lose this center imaging. Experiment with different distances to achieve the best possible sound.

As a speaker reproduces signals, especially bass reproduction, its enclosure often vibrates, diminishing the overall sound of the speaker. To minimize interior speaker vibration, consider purchasing some vibration dampening pads. Many speaker stands come equipped with these, but if your stands do not have them, you should consider investing.

You also need to consider how far the speakers are from the wall. The rear of the speaker should be at least twelve inches away from the wall. This becomes especially important when speakers feature rear ports, which allow sound and air to escape the inside of the speaker enclosure (they are then reflected by the rear wall). Moving the speakers closer to the wall can increase your bass response, but doing this may have adverse effects on other aspects of the sound, such as increased sound wave reflection from the rear wall.

The rear speakers require the least amount of setup. If possible, try to keep them at or slightly above ear level. Try different placements, such as on the sides of or behind the listening area, to see what works best for your room and speaker type. (See Figure 9.5.) If you have bookshelf speakers for your rear surround speakers, the placement will be similar to the front speaker placement. If you've chosen bipolar rear speakers, which output sound in two directions, try to keep them directly to the side of or directly behind the listening area, based on what you think sounds better.

Figure 9.5
Rear surround speakers should be beside or behind the listening area

The subwoofer's placement is most important. Placing your subwoofer in the corner may produce the loudest volume levels, but the overall quality and tightness of the bass may suffer due to the increased reflection of the sound waves. (See Figure 9.6.) Experiment with the subwoofer in a corner, and then place it to the side or behind the listening area. Unfortunately, subwoofers are large speakers and thus their placement may have to be less than optimal if aesthetics are a consideration. Try to identify possible locations for your subwoofer, and then experiment to determine which location works best in your setup.

The powered subwoofer moves a tremendous amount of air, thus the earth-shaking vibrations and sound. You should avoid placing objects directly in front, behind, or on top of the speaker until you know the objects are secure. Also, you may find that the subwoofer causes vibrations with items, such as blinds, pictures, and just about anything that isn't thoroughly nailed down. An annoying vibration can ruin the mood, so before inviting all your friends over to demo your new system, make sure you test out your system and eliminate those annoying rattles.

Figure 9.6
Placing your subwoofer in a corner can help increase its output, but the quality and tightness of the bass may suffer

Ported subwoofers are even more susceptible to positioning. A ported subwoofer features a port hole that allows sound and air to escape from inside the enclosure. When placing a ported subwoofer, ensure that you are not only pointing the speaker, but also give consideration to the port. For instance, don't place the port less than six inches from the wall. Ports need some distance from the wall to be effective.

Determining Setup Problems

The calibration discs help you know your speaker system is connected properly. The discs play sample audio signals and alert you to which speakers should be reproducing the signal. This is a quick and easy way to know your speakers are connected and that your DVD player is transferring audio to your receiver.

CHAPTER 9

The setup test patterns vary in complexity from the simple stereo (two-channel sound) to full Dolby Digital surround sound reproduction. The test tones often emanate from a single speaker at a time to allow you to pinpoint problems to a particular speaker. The tones also show the incredible power Dolby Digital has to send discrete signals to each of the five channels.

These setup tests can also help you identify "phase" problems. A speaker has positive and negative connections, and if these connections are reversed, the speaker is said to be operating "out of phase." If the speakers are not wired properly, the speaker system cannot place sounds in the sound field correctly, and imaging will be poor. Calibration discs often feature test signals that help identify if your speakers have been wired properly.

Understanding Reference Level

Reference level is the loudest possible output from your speakers when playing a selection. Reference level is 105 db while sitting in the primary listening area. This is the peak output level your system should hit when watching a DVD.

Calibration disc manufacturers recognize the need to set speakers to output reference level sounds, but they also realize that few listeners want to be subjected to 105 db volume. To solve this problem, manufacturers design calibration discs to step down the level at which their test tones are recorded. The amount of sound output volume below reference level varies from disc to disc, but the disc indicates the output level at which the disc was recorded. For instance, Avia is designed to calibrate to a signal of 85 dbs, or 20 decibels below peak level. Video Essentials is designed to calibrate to a signal of 75 dbs, or 30 decibels below peak level.

WARNING ABOUT CALIBRATION NOISE LEVELS

Even though calibration discs are set to levels lower than reference level, you may want to ensure that dogs and children are out of the house when you begin the calibration process, as test patterns are still quite loud, even at the reduced levels. When setting the subwoofer's volume level, be especially careful because the test tone vibrations may rattle unsecured objects.

Regardless of which calibration disc you use, the results should be the same. Both calibration discs give you the same result, a system that outputs a peak sound volume of 105 dbs. Keep in mind, though, that you do not have to listen to a movie at reference level; it is only meant to be a guide. Many people choose to listen to a lower volume level than reference level. I typically watch movies with my system outputting peak levels of 90 dbs.

To calibrate your system to reference level, first select a calibration DVD. For our purposes in this example, we use Avia, which was recorded at a level of 85 dbs. We, therefore, will calibrate the audio system to an output level of 85 dbs.

The first speaker to calibrate is the left-front speaker. Insert the calibration disc and navigate to the audio calibration portion of the disc. After the audio test signal from the calibration disc is playing, use a decibel meter to measure the speaker's output level. A single signal that is output only by the front-left speaker is the only sound output from this first test pattern. Adjust the receiver's volume level until the decibel meter reads 85 dbs.

HOW TO OBTAIN PROPER READINGS

Objects in your room reflect sound waves, including your body. A small camera tripod can help negate the reflection of sound from your body. Place the decibel meter on the tripod and stand just close enough to the tripod that you can still read the output gauge. If you don't have access to a tripod, just ensure that you hold the decibel meter at arm's length when taking readings.

After the speaker is outputting 85 decibels, make a note of your receiver's volume level, as this is your system's reference level. Do not adjust the volume level until you finish the calibration process. If you do accidentally change the volume level, return it to the level that you noted when it was at 85 dbs.

You may be wondering how you can adjust a speaker's output level without adjusting the volume on the receiver. Receivers can control each speaker's output level, independent of the receiver's volume level. Each receiver has a different way to adjust the speaker level, so be sure to consult your instruction manual to learn how to correctly set your system's speaker levels.

There is a misconception that reference level occurs when the receiver's volume level reaches a particular point. This is not necessarily true. Because of room and equipment differences (as discussed earlier in this chapter), the volume level required to output a 105 db peak output is different in each individual configuration. Even if you and your neighbor have the exact same receiver, the volume level required to produce a 105 db peak is likely to be different. Remember that reference level is the volume point on the receiver that produces a peak output of 105 dbs. The actual volume number on your receiver is insignificant and only needed if you plan on watching movies at reference level. The important thing is to get each of your speakers to produce the same output when given the same source from the calibration disc.

You are now ready to calibrate the right-front speaker. When the test signal begins, adjust the speaker level, not the volume level, of the right speaker until the decibel meter reads 85 dbs. If the speaker instantly reads 85 dbs, your two front speakers are already calibrated! If the meter reads higher or lower than 85, slowly adjust the level until the reading is 85 dbs.

ADJUST THE READINGS FOR OTHER DISCS

Keep in mind that the 85 decibel readings are specific to Avia. If using another calibration disc, listen to the introduction of the audio calibration sections to find the desired output level for that specific disc.

After your right- and left-front speakers have been properly calibrated, you are ready to calibrate the center channel speaker. Remember to finalize this speaker's placement before moving on to calibration. Follow the same process for your center speaker as you did for your front left and right speakers. Again, be sure to adjust the speaker level and not the volume level. After you obtain the desired output level from the center channel, the front three speakers have been properly calibrated and it is time to move on to the surround speakers and subwoofer.

You are now ready to calibrate the surround channel speakers. Use the same techniques as you did for the front three speakers and bring the surround channel speakers' output level up to the desired level. Don't be alarmed if each of your surround speakers requires different output levels; this is quite common due to room differences and acoustical differences, such as curtains, furniture, and doorways. The important part is that all speakers ultimately output the same decibel level when playing audio test patterns from the calibration disc. This guarantees that when you watch a DVD, the movie's soundtrack is reproduced at the appropriate level from each of the speakers in your system.

It doesn't matter which surround speaker you adjust first, just be sure to adjust them all. Most budget systems consist of two surround speakers, but if you have more than two, all your surround speakers need calibration. If your surround sound speakers are further away from your listening position than your main speakers, there is a good chance that you may have to raise their output level.

ADJUSTING OUTPUT LEVELS

In the rare case that you cannot reach the desired decibel reading with the speaker level adjustment, you may have to readjust the output level for all the other speakers. For example, if you have adjusted the gain on your right surround speaker to a maximum and still cannot reach the correct output level, you may need to reduce the speaker output levels on the other speakers to give yourself more adjustment range.

The subwoofer is the last speaker to calibrate, and its output level is subjective. Although you want your five satellite speakers outputting at the same level, you might want them to have a lower output level than your subwoofer. Many home theater enthusiasts do this because the low frequency effects created by the subwoofer make the experience even more real. Because the subwoofer re-creates only a small fraction of the audible sound spectrum, having a different output level is acceptable. The subwoofer typically runs five to ten decibels higher than the other speakers. For example, with an Avia disc, you might set your subwoofer to 90 dbs.

Calibrating you subwoofer is slightly different than calibrating your other speakers because a subwoofer has its own dedicated amplifier and crossover network. These differences make it easier to adjust your subwoofer to your desired output level. Although your receiver has a single volume control for five speakers, subwoofers have an independent volume control for a single speaker. This makes it easier to obtain the proper volume from the subwoofer. It is recommended that you set the receiver output level of the subwoofer to about 25% of the subwoofer level control. If the subwoofer level on your receiver ranges from –12 db to +12 db, a setting of –6 db is a good starting point. This ensures that the subwoofer receives the cleanest signal to its internal amplifier. Adjust the amplifier gain control and crossover settings to obtain the desired output level. You want to ensure that your crossover setting is at least 80 Hz. This is important because your receiver will be routing sounds below 80 Hz to your subwoofer. If you have a crossover setting of 50 Hz, you would effectively lose all the sounds between 50 Hz and 80 Hz. Remember to experiment with alternative placements of your subwoofer if it isn't performing to your expectations.

Try to derive a setting with a calibration disc, and then play one or more of the following selections to see if the bass output level is overpowering, just right, or not enough.

After you've found a starting point for your subwoofer, often the best way to finish dialing in your subwoofer settings is to listen to a real-world application, such as a DVD. The following are some great, bass-intensive scenes that give your subwoofer a workout. As you watch the passages, listen closely for distortion.

- Apollo 13. Scene 13
- Contact. Scene 33
- The Haunting. Scene 10
- The Matrix. Scene 31
- U-571. Scene 8

Professional Calibrations

If you are serious about extracting the most from your existing system and you've exhausted all the suggestions listed previously, you may consider getting your system professionally calibrated. The Imaging Science Foundation (ISF) has certified technicians who are skilled at advanced calibration techniques that far exceed the scope of basic tweaking.

ISF-certified technicians often travel across the country performing multiple calibrations in the same area on the same trip. This offers a more cost-effective price for the consumer by allowing multiple consumers in the same area to split travel cost.

Many of the ISF techniques involve removing the screen and working inside the television enclosure. Some ISF technicians use color analyzers to maximize your television's accuracy. Without a color analyzer, grayscale levels are difficult to set (and should not be attempted by the average user).

ISF calibration service varies in price depending on the level of calibration desired, the demand of the calibration technician, and your location. Check with your local high-end audio/visual retailers to see if they have an ISF-certified calibration technician on staff.

CHAPTER 9

10

Using Your System

This chapter is designed to help you make your new system easy to use. The best system in the world, after all, does you no good if you can't figure out how to use it. Sooner or later, you'll become frustrated if you have to go through ten steps on three remote controls every time you want to watch a movie. We help you sidestep that potential frustration by showing you how to consolidate your remote control commands, how to program user-friendly macros, how to simplify your setup by using your receiver's video-switching capability, and how to achieve optimal audio by selecting the best sound format for each type of audio signal. Now, let's get into the details for setting up and using your system.

Setting Your Remote to Control the Entire System

The first step to taking control of your home theater system is to consolidate your system's remotes. Although your receiver's remote is probably the only one with basic learning and macro capabilities, it might not be able to control your entire system. Most receiver remotes feature basic learning and macro creation capability, but they typically do not feature enough internal memory to completely reproduce the needed functionality from your other remote controls. Although it isn't realistic to transfer all the functionality from all your remotes into a single remote, it is almost a necessity that you get the basic functions funneled into a single remote.

First, identify the crucial buttons on each remote that you think you'll use regularly, such as:

▶ Channel Up/Down from the satellite receiver and/or television

▶ Play/Stop/Pause from the DVD player

▶ Volume Up/Down and Mute from the receiver

▶ Power On/Off for television, DVD player, satellite receiver, and VCR

If any of your remotes features preprogrammed codes for other devices, use the preprogrammed codes (as opposed to learning the new commands). See Figure 10.1. Your remote's preprogrammed codes do not use any additional memory, but learning infrared commands from another remote does—and it burns unused memory quickly. If a preprogrammed code isn't available, or if it doesn't work properly, don't be afraid to program the code. Just remember that your remote has limited memory capacity for learning new codes.

Figure 10.1
This remote, included with some Onkyo receivers, features preprogrammed codes and learning capability

If you've ever used a universal remote, you are probably familiar with preprogrammed codes. Most manufacturers use similar remote codes for their various components. For instance, often the same remote code works on two different Toshiba television models. Because remotes with preprogrammed codes store the codes in the remote's memory, all you must do is tell the remote what code you want to execute.

Programming Your Remote to Use Preprogrammed Codes

Now, let's walk through the process of programming your receiver's remote to use its preprogrammed codes. For this example, we use an Onkyo home theater remote control. Remember that the specific steps you need to follow to set up and use your remote's preprogrammed codes might differ from those in our example, but the procedure should be similar.

The first step in setting up a preprogrammed code for your receiver's remote is to identify the type and the brand of that device, such as a Panasonic television or a Pioneer DVD player. After you've identified the type and manufacturer, consult the remote control's manual (or the device that the remote control is associated with, such as the receiver). The manual should have a chart of preprogrammed codes for various devices. Table 10.1 shows what the preprogrammed codes in the manual should look like.

Table 10.1
Example of preprogrammed codes in a manual for televisions

Brand	Setting Number
Magnavox	162, 163
Mitsubishi	170, 171, 172, 173
Panasonic	187, 188, 189, 190
Philips	152, 162, 191
Toshiba	213, 229

As you can see in Table 10.1, numerous codes are listed for each of the different manufacturers. This is common, because manufacturers often have several code sets for their various models. If the device you are looking for has multiple code sets listed, try the first code listed after the brand name. If the first code doesn't seem to properly control your component, try the next code. For example, again in Table 10.1, if you input the Magnavox code 162 into the remote and your Magnavox television fails to respond, then you should try code 163.

Another thing to note in Table 10.1 is that sometimes different manufacturers use the same codes. For example, you can see that the preprogrammed code set 162 controls not only some Magnavox television sets, but also some Philips television sets. This is fairly common, because manufacturers often streamline basic functions, such as remote control commands, to lower production costs (by using existing remote control commands, companies don't have to spend research and development time and money coming up with new commands).

Now that you have identified the proper three-digit code, it is time to program it into your remote control. Again, the details differ among remotes, but the overall process is similar. The instruction manual included with your universal remote or receiver should give details on how to program in codes that will be used to control devices in your home theater system. For Onkyo's TX-DS595 remote, hold down the Mode button and press the Display button (while continuing to hold the Mode button). Then release both buttons. After you release the buttons, you have thirty seconds to key in the three-digit code to control your device. It's that simple for most remotes.

Test the remote after inputting your three-digit code. Begin by trying to power on the component. If it powers on, then try some basic remote control operations, such as Channel Up and Channel Down on a television or Play on a DVD player. If these work, you should then test the more advanced features, such as Picture-In-Picture Control on a television or the Menu button of your DVD player. If some but not all of the commands work, you can try one of the other codes listed in the instruction manual. You may find that one code works for some of your remote's functions but doesn't control all functions. If this occurs, your best alternative is to program the universal remote to learn the command from your existing remote.

Using Your Remote's Learning Ability

Universal remotes feature modes or devices that allow control of numerous components with a single remote. A typical universal remote has a mode or device for a television, a DVD player, a VCR, a satellite, and a CD player. A universal remote with learning ability can be used to overcome improper functioning with the preprogrammed codes on your component's remote. A remote that features learning ability "listens" to your original remote and copies the infrared signal sent by the original remote. The learning remote then stores this signal and reproduces it when the specific button is pressed.

Before you begin learning the command from another remote, you need to decide where you want to store the learned command (the button to be pressed to execute it). Try to pick a button with a label that helps you remember the command. Obviously, you are bound to confuse yourself and others if you change the command for Channel Up to Volume Up.

You most likely have to select the mode or device the button resides under. If you have the universal remote learn the Play button from your DVD player, it makes sense to use the DVD device button on the universal remote. Likewise, when programming your remote to learn a command from the television, you want to place that command under the remote's television mode.

After you identify the proper mode or device and button to learn (program) an IR (infrared) command into, it is time to physically learn (program) the command into the universal remote. Infrared is energy similar to light, but the wavelength is longer and invisible to the human eye.

INFRARED REMOTE CONTROLS

Most remotes use infrared signals to transmit commands to components. Infrared signals require "line of sight" to function properly. If an object is blocking the path between the remote and the component, the infrared signal does not work.

First, you need to find your remote's learning sensor. In most cases, this is on the tip of the remote in the same place from which the remote sends commands, but some remotes like the Philip's Pronto have a sensor located elsewhere, such as at the bottom of the remote. To get the universal remote to learn the command, position it four inches away from the original remote you are learning from (such as the DVD remote). Press the proper keys on the universal remote to get the universal remote ready to learn the new IR command. After getting the universal remote ready to learn the IR command, firmly press and release the button on the original remote. The original remote sends the command, the universal remote reads the command, stores it into its memory, and then allows replication of the command. You want to test the learned command to make sure it works properly. If the learned code does not function as it should, then repeat the process of teaching the remote to try to get a clean learned code that operates properly. If you continue to have problems, be sure you haven't exceeded your memory limit. If your remote is out of memory, it will not learn more commands.

Your remote's or receiver's owner's manual should explain the "learning" process in depth. Most learning remotes use a series of blinking lights to indicate if the codes have been learned properly (or if they have failed). Often, if the learning process fails, the number of blinks from the light indicates the problem. For example, the following steps are needed to teach a remote command into the Radio Shack 15-1994 remote control.

1. Press and hold the Setup Button until the red LED (light) flashes twice.

2. Press 9, then press 7, then press 5. The red LED will flash twice.

3. Press the DEVICE key (for example, the DVD key) where you want to teach the command into.

4. Press the button you want to learn the function into (for example, the Power button).

5. Press the button on the original remote that you want to teach into the Radio Shack remote.

6. If the teaching process was successful, the LED will flash once. If the LED flashes multiple times, the code was not properly learned and the process will need to be repeated.

If you do run out of memory before your universal remote learns all the essential commands, you may be forced to reinitialize your remote. Most universal remotes allow you to format their memory, giving you a clean slate from which to start. If you have used all your remote control's memory, you can estimate how many buttons the remote can learn. After you've obtained an estimate for the amount of buttons you can learn, you can reevaluate the "essential" buttons. If your remote doesn't have the capability to learn all the buttons you need to properly control your system, you will probably be best served to upgrade the remote to a more capable remote control.

Programming Macros to Perform Common Tasks

Think about how many times you've turned all your components on and off. Wouldn't it be great if you could turn off your television, DVD player, home theater receiver, and satellite receiver all with the push of one button? Well, this is exactly the sort of thing a macro button can do for you. A macro button is programmed to perform a series of steps with the press of a button. Macros transform a complicated but well-set up system into an easy-to-use system. You (and the whole family) are sure to get more use out of a system that is easy to use.

Macros should be the final step in setting up your remote control, performed after the first two steps (using preprogrammed codes and learning codes from existing remotes) have been completed. Some remotes limit the number of commands that each macro can execute, so be sure each step is essential if you are having problems programming a macro to the remote.

The most common macros allow you to turn the system on and off with the press of one button, but there are more macros you should consider using. First, try to note all common functions you repeatedly use. I personally use macros to switch from a satellite source to a DVD source and to power the system on and off. You'll want to simplify your system so every member of the family can control the basic tasks, such as turning on the system, watching cable television, selecting a DVD movie, and shutting off the system. If you can program these macros into your system, it becomes much easier to use.

To program a macro into a remote control, you must identify all buttons to be pushed and in what order they should be activated. The easiest way to do this is to write each button's name and command on a sheet of paper before you begin actually inputting the commands into the remote. After you've taken notes about the series of commands you want to use in a macro button, identify the mode and button on the remote that needs to be accessed. This creates a detailed list of the button combinations that control the macro. The following is a sample command list for a macro to power on the system and to switch the receiver to satellite television.

1. Turn Television Power On—Receiver Remote Mode TV, Power button
2. Turn Receiver Power On—Receiver Remote Mode Receiver, Power button
3. Turn Satellite Receiver Power On—Receiver Remote Mode Sat, Power button
4. Turn Television to Input #1—Receiver Remote Mode TV, Input button
5. Turn the Receiver to Satellite Receiver Output—Receiver Remote, Sat Input button

As you can see in the previous numbered list, five steps are required to view satellite television. Considering that each step requires pressing a Mode button followed by another action button, this process requires approximately ten buttons to be pressed in the right order every time you sit down to watch television. By programming these into a macro, you can accomplish the same thing by pressing one or two buttons. Some remotes have a button that must be pressed to activate a macro command, followed by the number of the macro you want to perform. Other remotes may have several dedicated buttons that perform a macro command by pressing only one button.

Teaching macro commands differs for various remote controls. For demonstration purposes, we walk through setting up the macro commands listed in the previous numbered list on a remote included with most Onkyo budget home theater receivers.

The Onkyo remote allows a single macro for each mode or device listed on the remote control. As you can see in Figure 10.2, there are eight modes available on this remote. For ease of remembering, we program the Power On macro into the Direct Macro button. This button executes a macro with a single button press, instead of having to press a mode or device followed by the Mode macro button. Because the Power On macro will likely be the most heavily used macro, we use the macro button labeled 1 for this macro command.

Figure 10.2
Mode buttons allow the contol of multiple devices using a single remote control

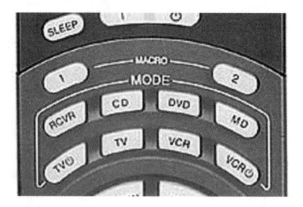

DIRECT MACRO BUTTON

Your remote may not have a button labeled Direct Macro, but it may have a button that performs the same function. The Direct Macro button is essentially just a macro command free of mode or device. It is meant to be used system-wide, instead of being geared toward a single mode or device in the system.

To program one of the macro buttons on the Onkyo remote, hold down any one of the mode buttons and then press the Direct Macro button. After pressing the Direct Macro button, release both buttons. At this point, you are ready to begin inputting the steps in the macro. First, press the TV mode button followed by the On button. Next, press and release the Receiver mode button and then press the On button. Repeat the process for the satellite receiver. After you finish inputting the remaining button combinations, press the Direct Macro button to complete the procedure.

After you finish programming a macro button, test it. Keep in mind that the remote is going to be sending multiple commands, so the testing process may take several seconds (and you therefore must continue to keep the remote pointed in the direction of your components). Also, remember that your television and satellite receivers, as well as your home theater receiver, will receive IR signals, so be sure to point the remote in their direction so their devices can receive the signal.

Understanding Discrete Codes

So, you've just gotten your Power On macro completed and are ready to test it. But just when you push the macro button, someone walks right in front of you and your remote. Well, now your television and receiver are on, but the satellite receiver isn't. If you run the Power On macro again, you'll likely end up with the satellite receiver on, but the television and receiver off. That's where discrete codes come into play.

Discrete codes send a command that only performs a designated function regardless of the component's state. For instance, on a home theater receiver remote, you have a power button. If you press the power button while the receiver is on, the receiver turns off, but if the power button sent a discrete "On" command, the receiver would remain on. A discrete power command turns the receiver on if the receiver is off, but if the receiver is on, sending the discrete power command does nothing.

Although this may not sound like a vital feature, it can be very handy when building macro commands. Think about the situation in which someone walks in front of you as the macro is executing. If you had discrete commands, you could simply reissue the Power On command, and the devices that were on would remain on and the device that failed to power on would then be turned on. Discrete commands help make your macro commands foolproof.

Before you get too excited about discrete codes, I've got to give you the bad news. Not all devices have discrete codes programmed into them, and if your device doesn't come with discrete codes, there isn't much you can do about it. The bad news doesn't stop there either, because many devices that do have discrete codes only have a few discrete codes, not the entire remote control command set.

So, how do you find out if your devices have discrete codes? You can send correspondence to your manufacturer, but you might have to wait weeks for a response. I suggest you take advantage of information available on the Internet. There are many websites with reviews and information about remote controls. The best of them is www.RemoteCentral.com, a comprehensive site about all things related to remote controls. The site has a database of all available discrete codes that thousands of users have discovered for various components.

Using Your Receiver's Video-Switching Capability

Your receiver is the central hub of your system, possessing features that can help simplify controlling your system. As discussed in Chapter 8, you can choose to route your video signals through your receiver or directly to your video monitor. If you route the cables through your receiver, you have many video inputs that are connected to the receiver, and a single video output that is connected to the video monitor. If you choose to route the video signals directly to the video monitor, you have many video inputs that are connected to the television. Although video purists recommend routing the video signals directly to the monitor, I recommend using your receiver to do the video switching, especially if you're trying to simplify your system's operation.

So, how does using your receiver's video switching help simplify operation? Consider how your system functions if you have the DVD player's video signal and the satellite receiver's video signal running directly into the television monitor. Think about the number of remote control commands you need to execute when switching from watching satellite television to watching a DVD. First, you need to get the television to its correct input. Then, you have to get the receiver to the correct input. This synchronization can be confusing for novice users, and it adds complexity to macro commands.

If your system is set up to use the receiver's video-switching capabilities, the process is easier. A single button switches the audio source and the video source, ensuring that the audio and video signals are always in synch. With this setup, your television monitor stays on the same input regardless of the source being used. This small setup difference makes system operation much easier for you, especially if all the buttons on a remote control intimidate you.

Another advantage to using your receiver for video-switching is that the receiver's remote often has easy access to switching the audio and video inputs. Also, because of the one-button access to different sources, you can avoid the need for programming macro commands to switch between sources. Using your receiver for video switching creates macro commands for changing input sources, which is quite useful if you have chosen to use the remote included with your home theater receiver.

Although some may argue that routing video signals through the receiver degrades the video signal quality, I disagree. I've never detected a noticeable quality difference when routing video signals through the receiver or directly to the television monitor. That said, some definite drawbacks do exist. If, for example, your receiver only supports S-Video switching and you want to use component video connections, you are forced to route the component video signals directly to the television. Another drawback is that most receivers can only output the same type of video signal that is being input into the receiver. For example, if you have only composite video connections from your VCR, most receivers are only able to output a composite signal to the television. Few budget receivers possess the ability to "upconvert" a composite signal to an S-Video signal. In this case, you are then forced to run an S-Video cable from your video source to your television. This leads to added cable length, which ultimately affects your budget. If you are forced—or simply choose—to use your television for video-switching purposes, you can minimize the complexity of this approach. For instance, you can program a macro command that switches the video input on the television, like in the examples presented earlier in this chapter in the "Programming Macros to Perform Common Tasks" section.

Managing Your Cables

When you imagine your dream system, you likely envision the components but not the many cables that connect them. Although you shouldn't worry too much about cable management when you initially hook up your system, after you become comfortable with the arrangement of wires, you should make a point to organize them. A poorly-wired system can leave an immediate bad first impression on potential viewers, including family members, and it can wreak havoc on you when something goes wrong and you can't figure out which cable goes where.

Many audio component racks and stands not only give you a good place to store and display your numerous home theater components, but they also have integrated cable management. Although the cable management differs for each, the goal is always the same: to organize the cables.

If you plan to purchase an audio and video component rack, consider the audio rack's cable management properties before you buy. The audio rack should conceal the cables. Also, make sure that you can route the power cables from your devices away from the interconnect cables that send signals between the devices in your home theater system. Many audio racks offer cable management schemes that all but force you to route all the cables in your system tightly together. Although this makes the appearance of your system look good and neatly organized, it can introduce unwanted interference.

If you don't plan to use an audio rack, there are alternative ways to organize cables. An inexpensive way to organize cables is to use plastic zip ties to bundle cables together. Remember to group power cords together, away from the cords carrying audio and video signals. It is a good idea to start organizing with the component that is highest from the ground, because it has the longest cables.

Cable length is also important. As discussed in Chapter 8, you obtain the right cable length by using a string. The string lets you simulate how the actual cable will be placed, and gives you a good estimate of the needed length. You'll want to ensure that you run the string in the same path the actual cable will run. If needed, use tape to secure one end of the string to one connection point while you route the string to the other connection point. It's much easier to conceal a three-foot cable than a twelve-foot cable. Of course, you must leave a little "play" by making sure your cables are long enough to move your components without having to disconnect your devices.

You should also label each cable. Several companies sell small labeling kits that help take the guesswork out of determining which cable goes where. These labels simply attach to your interconnect cables with a small tag that displays something like "DVD" or "TV Video Output." The labels can be especially helpful if you want to rewire your system but are concerned about getting everything reconnected properly. Use the labels to make sure you understand where each connection goes, and then disconnect your wires. After you've organized your cables, reconnecting your system should be simple.

Cable management is also helpful when you upgrade your system. If you have to untangle a large mess of cables, the upgrade is likely to be more frustrating and time-consuming, but if your system's cables are organized and labeled, the upgrade is typically quick and painless.

CHAPTER 10

Selecting the Right Audio Format

To obtain peak performance out of your audio system, you must have the correct audio format selected. Your receiver tries to help you by storing the last sound field you selected for each input, so you need to make sure you have the correct sound field selected for each input. A DVD movie is much more impressive and realistic when played back in Dolby Digital or DTS than in two-channel stereo sound.

You want to pick the top audio format that the signal presents. For example, I've mentioned that Dolby Digital and DTS are the best audio formats available, and should be chosen (when available). However, when these aren't available, you need to select another sound format, such as Dolby Pro Logic II.

The following chart lists the suggested sound format for several different types of audio signals. Remember, these are only guidelines and suggestions; if you prefer a sound format other than the one suggested, use it.

Table 10.2
Suggested audio formats

Signal	Suggested Format
Standard cable	Dolby Pro Logic II
Digital cable	Dolby Digital (if available) or Dolby Pro Logic II
HDTV	Dolby Digital
DVD	DTS (when available), Dolby Digital (DTS ES or Dolby Digital EX if your system supports this)
VCR tapes	Dolby Pro Logic II
Satellite broadcast	Dolby Pro Logic (some pay-per-view movies feature Dolby Digital)
CD	Dolby Pro Logic II or Two-Channel Stereo
AM/FM radio	Dolby Pro Logic II or Two-Channel Stereo

After you get the correct sound format for each input on your home theater receiver, you shouldn't have to worry about the format again unless you change it manually. The receiver remembers that you prefer DVDs to run Dolby Digital but your CD to run Dolby Pro Logic II.

Many people have problems getting their home theater system to play back a DTS surround sound track. If you are having problems getting sound from a DTS sound track, make sure both your DVD player and your home theater receiver support DTS signals. You should see the DTS logo on the front of your DVD player and home theater receiver; if not, consult your owner's manual to find out if DTS is supported. (See Figure 10.3.)

Figure 10.3
As you can see, the
Onkyo TX-DS500 home
theater receiver
supports the DTS
surround format

If both devices support the DTS surround sound format, then check the setup menu of your
DVD player. Many times, DTS output is disabled by default in the DVD player's menu. If the
signal is not being output, change the setting to output the DTS signal. Your receiver should
automatically recognize the DTS signal and switch to DTS mode when the DVD player sends a
DTS digital bitstream to it. If your receiver doesn't recognize the signal, try cycling through the
surround sound formats on the receiver until you see the DTS signal is detected and your hear
sound coming from the speakers.

11
The Upgrade Path

Even the most well-planned system eventually needs to be updated. This chapter is dedicated to helping you recognize which components will stay with you for years and which will likely be the first to need replaced. A quality set of loudspeakers, for example, will likely withstand the test of time much better than a home theater receiver (not because the receiver is inferior but because receiver technology changes much faster than speaker technology). By building a system properly and thinking about eventual upgrades upfront, you can minimize future costs. I also introduce you to the world of separates, which are found in virtually every high-end audio system. If your system has been built properly, the jump from a home theater receiver to separates should be simple and rewarding.

The first thing home theater owners want to upgrade is their sound system; they want to upgrade to obtain the most current, best sound available. If you've done your homework, making an audio upgrade should be simple, but if you haven't and own a poorly compiled system, you may not only have trouble upgrading, but it could also be very costly. That's the problem with the "home theater in a box"; it's less expensive in the short term but a burden in the long term, because it is often difficult, if not impossible, to upgrade only a single component in the system. You have to buy a completely new system or settle for what you already own.

How to Maximize Your Upgrade Dollars

If and when you decide to give your existing system a little boost, you'll want to spend your upgrade dollars wisely. Although speakers are an easy item to replace, your upgrade dollars will probably be better spent on another part of your system. For instance, if you have a Dolby Pro Logic receiver, it is better for you to upgrade to a Dolby Digital and DTS capable receiver than to replace your speakers. When upgrading your home theater system, you want to identify the weakest link in your system and replace that component first.

Identifying the Weakest Link

Everyone has heard the adage that a chain is only as strong as its weakest link. Keep that in mind with your home theater system—one weak link can damage all other strong components because they all must work together to create the home theater experience. If your receiver doesn't send a clean, powerfully amplified signal to your speakers, they will produce an inferior sound that is below their capacity. In that case, you want to make sure you know your receiver is the problem, instead of assuming it's your speakers. That's why it's so important when upgrading to determine the "weakest link," the component that needs replaced first. This section helps you figure that out.

If you've followed the tips and advice in Home Theater Solutions, upgrading is simple. That's because this book recommends that you invest more money up front in a quality surround sound speaker system than on other components. The reasoning behind this is simple: Your speakers will outlast the rest of your home theater components. Although this places some pressure on you to select a quality speaker system up front, the rewards are worth it in the long run.

Upgrading Your Home Theater Receiver

Your home theater receiver will likely be the first component you need to replace. Because home theater receivers are the brains of the system, processing and decoding many signals, you want to make sure it's current. If a new surround sound format is introduced and your receiver can't process it, you may want to improve your overall sound by upgrading to a receiver that can process the new format.

Another reason your home theater receiver likely will be the first item you replace is the continual feature and performance migration from the high-end receivers to the budget receivers. Unless money was no option when you bought your receiver, chances are that there was probably another, much more expensive receiver on the market that offered more amplification power and other features not found in your receiver. Well, the good news is that as receivers evolve, the lower-end budget models will offer features and performance previously found only in costly high-end models. (See Figure 11.1.) Unless you absolutely have to be on the cutting edge, this is a great way to enjoy your home theater without breaking the bank.

Figure 11.1
The new Onkyo TX-DS600 is a powerful home theater receiver with an impressive feature list for the price

A great example of this trickle-down effect on features and performance is a receiver's component video switching capabilities. Component video switching requires inputting at least two component video sources, such as an HDTV signal, to the receiver and having the receiver pass the video signal through to the television monitor. In last year's budget home theater receiver, very few receivers featured component video switching. However, this year, several new budget-oriented receivers not only feature component video switching, but also have six channels of amplification for Dolby Digital EX and DTS ES surround sound formats. Often, you'll find the features that you wanted when you bought your first home theater receiver have migrated down from the more expensive receivers into the budget models. If you don't want to spend several hundred dollars more just for a couple extra features, buy the less expensive receiver for now and upgrade in a couple of years when the features become standard in the budget receivers. You can't be on the cutting edge of technology on a tight budget.

Upgrading Your DVD Player

If your receiver is still faithfully performing up to par, then it's time to look at replacing another component, which will likely be your DVD player. As with a home theater receiver, a DVD player features a considerable amount of technology, and that technology is always evolving; there's inevitably some new feature "in the works." Perhaps when you bought your DVD player, you decided to save money and passed on that DVD player with DVD-Audio capability and progressive scan video output. Well, chances are the player that you passed on can now be found at a much lower price.

DVD player prices have fallen dramatically, to the point that they are quite affordable and many households have one. With such widespread acceptance of DVD players, you can rest assured that this technology will be around for years. New DVD features and standards continue to emerge—recent developments include progressive scan and DVD-Audio discs playback—and if your DVD player isn't up to par with others on the market, you might want to upgrade.

Upgrading the DVD player is common with home theater owners, especially if you desire having a DVD player in another room, such as a bedroom or office. Also, when thinking about upgrading or replacing your DVD player, remember that many of today's video game consoles, such as the Microsoft Xbox and Sony's Playstation 2, can function as DVD players. Although these players don't offer features found on high-end DVD players, the quality is acceptable, especially when using a 40-inch or smaller television.

Upgrading Your Television

If you have extra money, but don't want the hassle associated with setting up a new piece of equipment, you might consider upgrading your television monitor. The television monitor is a simple piece of equipment to upgrade. If you are using the receiver for video switching, it may be as easy as plugging in the power cord and connecting a single video output from the receiver.

When upgrading the television, look for whether it displays progressive scan images and HDTV signals. These features continue to trickle down to more affordable sets, but still require a substantial increase in price over a similar set without these features. When looking for a set, try to find one that will display a 480p signal as well as a 1080i signal.

Of course, when upgrading the television, the first thought always seems to be that one should get the biggest television possible. This isn't always the best decision. Let's first look at an example from a rear projection television set (RPTV). Most manufacturers today offer sets in various sizes from forty inches to sixty-five inches in diagonal length. Often, these various-sized sets have similar electronics inside their cabinets. Standard definition (480i) cable sources are not high-quality video sources, and when these images are enlarged for display on a large-screen television, the quality suffers. This means that a forty-inch television and a sixty-five inch television from the same model line will likely output differing image qualities. The forty-inch television most likely provides better image quality. The larger screen format shows the imperfections of the video signal more because it displays the image on a bigger screen. The image on the larger television is bigger, of course, but won't necessarily be better because of the low-quality signal delivered by standard definition sources.

This shortcoming of large-screen televisions is minimized when used with higher signal quality, such as those produced by DVD movies and HDTV signals. With more lines of resolution, the overall picture being displayed is dramatically improved and the quality of the larger monitor is closer to that of a smaller one. More lines of resolution create a more accurate image too, which helps to create a greater sense of depth. Often, when people view an HDTV signal for the first time, they are pleasantly shocked by the image's incredible clarity and three-dimensionality. Of course, if you can live with the less-than-perfect image that standard definition cable and satellite broadcasts offer, a larger-screen television will still work for you.

Another option when upgrading your television monitor is to look at a flat-display television. A flat-display television, such as Sony's Wega series, offers an exceptionally sharp picture, especially in the corners of the screen. Many flat-display television sets also offer features that enhance DVD playback (for an even better picture).

These flat-display television sets get confused with the thin plasma displays recently introduced to consumers. These flat-display sets being referred to are similar in size to a typical CRT tube-based television monitor, but they offer flat front glass, unlike a conventional, curved-front CRT tube-based monitor.

The advantage of the flat-display sets is that you get the easy operation and maintenance of a tube television, but you also get the flat display (like a rear projection or plasma display). The disadvantage of the flat-display set is primarily cost. For example, a standard 32-inch Toshiba television with a typical curved-front glass display has a retail price of about $600. A flat-display 32-inch Toshiba television has a retail price of almost $950. Another disadvantage is that no manufacturer makes a flat-display television larger than thirty-six inches. Those looking for a large-screen television will likely have to look toward a rear projection television set.

Upgrading Your Cables

Cables are often overlooked, but they need to be upgraded, too. Remember that cables connect devices and deliver sound to the speakers. If your signals are losing signal quality, then your system is surely not performing at its best. When initially building your system, you likely skimped on your cables so you could buy the components you really desired. Although this is a valid strategy, cables should not be ignored when you begin to upgrade.

Ask any audiophile how much he spends on cables, and you'll likely be shocked. Many high-end cables can be incredibly expensive, but they're becoming more affordable, as many well-respected cable manufacturers are emerging on the Internet offering quality cables at inexpensive prices. These manufacturers don't sell their cables in your local store, but may be able to provide you with a higher quality cable at a lower price. Many, including myself, view these cables as a much better option than the high-end Monster cables that Best Buy and other large electronics stores carry (and often push to consumers). Monster cables are usually more expensive than a similar cable from the Internet vendors. I've had much better reliability with cables from Internet vendors than with Monster cables. The major drawback to buying high-end cables from the Internet vendors, like BetterCables.com, is that you may have to wait because most cables are custom-made for each customer.

Your system relies on many cables, so don't expect to upgrade them all without spending a considerable amount of money. A good strategy is to upgrade the video cables first, then—when your budget allows—upgrade the audio and speaker cables. FYI: Cheap video cables don't last as long as cheap audio cables.

Cable preference is subjective, as is receiver and speaker preference. However, most value-oriented experts agree that expensive cables sold at the big chain electronics stores are not the best cables to purchase. If you plan to upgrade your cables, I suggest using a direct-to-consumer cable company. Although there are many quality cable companies to consider, www.BolderCables.com, www.CatCables.com, and www.BetterCables.com are three top choices by many home theater enthusiasts.

Upgrading Your Remote Control

An increasingly popular upgrade to a home theater system is a better, more capable universal remote control. As mentioned in Chapter 8, universal remotes can help ease the burden of learning a complicated system, allowing less technical people to use a home theater system.

One of the most advanced universal remote controls is the Philip's Pronto. The Pronto is a touch-screen LCD remote that is almost infinitely configurable and customizable. The Pronto allows you to create customized screens that you can design on your home computer. Commands from other remotes are then programmed into the layouts. The Pronto features a tremendous amount of memory that allows control of very complex systems. Some manufacturers, such as Onkyo, like the Pronto remote so much that they have chosen to repackage it and include it with their high-end receivers. Onkyo, for instance, has dubbed their version of the Pronto the CHAD, or Custom Home Automation Device. See Figure 11.2.

Figure 11.2
The Philip's Pronto and the Onkyo CHAD both have the ability to create a custom graphic user interface; both are also almost infinitely configurable and customizable

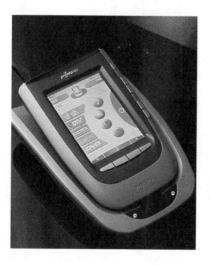

Another benefit of the Pronto and similar graphic remotes is its ability to develop custom button layouts. You will like this feature, as you tend to use certain buttons more than others. You can also customize the size, shape, look, and label of each button.

Of course, the Pronto is not for everyone. It is expensive, and not everyone likes the touch screen. Moreover, many home theater users do not want to spend time designing their custom layouts. If you're one such person, don't fret, because you have many other options.

When selecting a remote control, ensure that it has learning and macro capabilities, coupled with a large amount of memory. Without question, you'll certainly have to learn some keys to accomplish complete control of your system.

By investing in a capable universal remote, you may also be able to further simplify your setup by creating more complex macro commands. High-end remote controls offer incredible options for programming macros and can make operating your system much easier. Although these remotes may seem very expensive, they're also good investments—this is one device that you can keep and use for many years, regardless of the other components in your system.

Upgrading Your Powered Subwoofer

The first component in your speaker system to be upgraded should probably be the powered subwoofer. Although the signal that a subwoofer receives is limited, its impact on the overall sound is arguably the most noticeable. The subwoofer is usually easy to upgrade because it is typically connected by a single interconnect cable. Powered subwoofers are also easy to blend in with an existing speaker system, which makes the subwoofer a favorite among home theater owners looking to upgrade.

So, what should you look for when upgrading your subwoofer? The first thing you should look for is to increase the overall wattage of the powered subwoofer and increase the quality. I recommend staying with a subwoofer that has a driver no larger than twelve inches in diameter. Some manufacturers make powered subwoofers with fifteen-inch drivers, but bigger isn't always better.

Several direct-to-consumer manufacturers have created some incredible powered subwoofers. I recommend checking into subwoofer offerings from HSU Subwoofers, SVS Subwoofers, and Aperion Audio. These companies specialize in making subwoofers that outperform more expensive models. These products have a tremendous following on numerous Internet message boards; home theater enthusiasts sing praises for these products continuously. Having personal experience with products from these vendors, I am also a firm believer that these companies are making incredible home theater products that are real bargains.

What to Do With Your Old Stuff

Many home theater owners wonder what they will do with their old component(s). Often, you can soften the blow of upgrading by selling your old components and applying the earnings towards the purchase of your new components. Many online auction sites offer good prices for used equipment, and with the explosion of online shopping, there are many potential buyers waiting.

Although selling is an option that can increase your overall budget for upgrading, many people also opt to keep their existing equipment and use it in another room. If you are upgrading your television monitor, it's often useful to put your existing television in another room, such as a bedroom. Another good idea for an old receiver is to use it in conjunction with your home computer to make a powerful, digital music jukebox that can store digital copies of all your CDs.

Speakers can either be sold or used for another purpose. A high-quality set of speakers can turn a computer into an equally high-quality jukebox. Computer games take on new life when combined with a great sound system. You'll be hard-pressed to find a set of computer speakers that perform as well as your old home theater speakers.

Continuously Changing Technology

If there is a constant in the world of home theater, it is that the technology is always changing. It never fails, of course, that at about the time you've made up your mind to buy a new receiver, an even newer model is announced, possessing a few more features but costing many more dollars. This can be confusing and frustrating, putting you in a dilemma: Do you stick with the receiver you've had your heart set on for months or do you buy the just-released model? I can't decide for you and I can't "future proof" your home theater purchases, but I can offer some suggestions for buying at the right time and upgrading for the right reasons.

You probably know that every product released is touted as "ground-breaking" and a "must have" for all home theater consumers. That's the nature of the advertising beast. But, especially in home theater, it can be difficult to distinguish worthy improvements and new handy features from mere hype. Be leery of the hype and of a manufacturer's persuasive ad campaign, which tries to convince you that a new product is crucial to your home theater experience—usually it is not. An example of this was the much-hyped release of Dolby Pro Logic II. Whether to invest in this new surround sound format was a widely debated issue on Internet message boards: Is it worth spending the money to upgrade to Dolby Pro Logic II? Is my almost new, only one year-old receiver obsolete because it doesn't support the Dolby Pro Logic II format?

Dolby Pro Logic II was an improvement over the original Dolby Pro Logic format. But it was hardly a major breakthrough in home theater, unlike, say, Dolby Digital, which was released in 1992. Dolby Pro Logic II hit the home theater scene in 2001. Although it wasn't meant to be a competitor for superior digital surround sound formats like Dolby Digital and DTS, the marketing campaign was heavy. And it worked. A buying frenzy ensued in 2001, as many home theater users rushed to upgrade to a new receiver with Dolby Pro Logic II capability. Although the upgrade certainly gave new life to older Dolby Pro Logic encoded material, it didn't make the lasting impression that Dolby Digital has had. Dolby Digital was quite revolutionary for home theaters, the first "true" all digital discrete surround sound format that brought a movie theater's high-quality sound into homes. Dolby Pro Logic II was not revolutionary; it simply improved on an existing technology that has been commonplace in home theater systems for years. So, did everyone who upgraded their receivers to get Dolby Pro Logic II throw their money away? Absolutely not, but they may have been better off—especially if money was an issue—letting the technology gain some mainstream acceptance before buying into it.

The inevitable question follows: How do you differentiate between an overly-hyped marketing blitz and a worthy new feature? The best advice I can give is to be patient. Early adopters of a product are often folks who love the latest and greatest buzzwords and gadgets, and so they buy everything when it comes out, regardless of its worth. I suggest you resist the temptation to purchase something that's just been released; let the masses test and evaluate it. Then, you'll get a good idea of whether the buzz about the product is hype or legitimate praise. Often, it is better to pass on a first-generation model of a new component or format and wait for the second offering. By waiting for the second generation, you get a more reliable (trouble-free) product. Plus, the price will likely be cheaper as well. Never rush into a buying decision—the component will still be there if you decide to buy it after it's proven itself.

Another way to avoid buying into marketing ploys is to educate yourself about the product. Read reviews in magazines, talk to your local dealer, and browse Internet message boards. Keep in mind when reading reviews, though, that the reviewer's opinion isn't the only opinion. Also remember that dealers want to sell their new items, so they might encourage you to buy a new product even if you don't need it. Although you never know who's who on Internet message boards, you do get a variety of opinions, as thousands of home theater consumers gather daily to discuss the merits and drawbacks of home theater technology. And that's the best way to get informed and make up your own mind about a product. Scour the wealth of differing opinions on a given product (read all the "this is a must have" and "this is junk" material you can), as this allows you to read and evaluate the opinions of regular home theater users.

A trend you'll quickly notice in home theater gear is the trickling down of features. If the feature you want is only available on the high-end, high-priced component, consider waiting for the next year's models to be announced and see if the feature has been trickled down into the other models, which is likely. Manufacturers commonly move high-end features to lower-end models to recoup research and development costs, and to provide a greater feature set in their budget models.

Moving to a High-End System

If you've quickly outgrown your budget home theater system and are looking to build a high-end system, there are several things to consider. If your budget has expanded, or if you are looking to make a more long-term home theater investment, you should consider upgrading to a few high-end components. These are found in high-end systems, those that are often dedicated home theater rooms. Hence, they are not used for everyday television viewing but for home theater (movie) watching. High-end systems can consist of receivers and amplifiers that cost several thousand dollars each. These high-end systems are the ultimate in home theater entertainment, but the price tag associated with building a high-end, dedicated theater room makes them unobtainable for the average consumer.

Separates

Many high-end systems consist of "separates." Separates is a term used to describe the process of separating the amplification component from the processing component. Separates systems are also sometimes called "Pre/Pro" systems. A home theater receiver not only processes incoming signals, but it also amplifies the output signal to the speaker. A separates system features two units: a processing unit that only processes the audio and video signals being input from the home theater components (such as a DVD player), and an amplification component that amplifies the output signals to the speakers.

Systems that use separate components are expensive, but they deliver a higher quality of sound than a budget system. If you are serious about your home theater system, separates could be the next upgrade for you.

Separates offer an increased level of flexibility as well. This is because the processing unit and amplification unit can be upgraded independent of each other. Even if the surround sound formats rapidly change, for instance, the amplifier will be unaffected because it only amplifies and does no signal processing. That means the amp will last for years. Also, because amplifier units consist of individual power supplies, they can output increased amounts of power even under heavy loads common with scenes from DVD movies. But, again, it's hard to justify the high price tag. Buying a preamplifier processor and an amplification unit will cost you several thousand dollars.

High-End Receivers

If you aren't ready to commit to a system with separates, a high-end receiver could be the upgrade that suits you (see Figure 11.3). Many receivers deliver lots of power and contain loads of highly useful features. Denon and Onkyo are two companies that make upgradeable receivers, so your large investment can keep up with changing standards and formats.

These top-of-the-line receivers are the flagship models for each manufacturer. They include all the most advanced features and the cleanest, most powerful amplifiers available. These receivers also are usually THX certified, ensuring the best quality you can get in a home theater receiver.

Figure 11.3
High-end receivers, like the Onkyo TX-DS989, provide great performance

Front Projection

Another upgrade typically found in high-end systems is a projector. Although projectors require a lot of planning and labor on your end—because most projection units need to be suspended from the ceiling—they do offer incredibly high-quality pictures on large screens (often over one-hundred inches in size). Projectors continue to become more popular in home theaters, as the technology develops and prices drop. But they are still relatively expensive. (See Figure 11.4.) You also need to purchase a screen, of course, which adds to the overall cost of the system. Another drawback of projectors is the cost of replacement bulbs. A typical bulb for a front projection lasts only about 1,000 hours and can cost hundreds of dollars.

Figure 11.4

A front projection
system is a great way to
get high-quality video,
but cost is usually
prohibitive for those on
a budget

Every home theater system is going to need an upgrade sooner or later. However, if you plan ahead, take your time, and educate yourself, you will upgrade at the right time. Don't buy into all the marketing hype, and make sure that the new feature is really worth paying for, that it will really add to your home theater set up.

Appendix A
Web Yellow Pages of Useful Home Theater Sites

The key to making wise purchasing decisions is to be informed when shopping. Fortunately, the Internet has opened up a world of information for you, the consumer, but you've got to know where to look to find the right information. Appendix A offers you my recommended list of helpful home theater websites.

Product Review Sites

Read a couple of message boards and you'll quickly realize there are a lot of passionate home theater enthusiasts just waiting to push their favorite products on you. Although such folks usually have good, legitimate reasons for recommending these products, you have no way of knowing if the person touting a product possesses the credentials and objectivity for spouting off such opinions. It's not surprising, by the way, for manufacturers to post laudatory messages about their products, all of course in the guise of anonymity. That's why you shouldn't rely on one opinion or even one site. Independent review sites offer a wide variety of home theater equipment reviews, giving you a good idea of where to start your search. The following sections list some of my favorites.

CheapHomeTheater.com

If you are looking for the best home theater components for your money, CheapHomeTheater.com (http://www.CheapHomeTheater.com) is the site. As the editor of CheapHomeTheater.com, I've had the opportunity to discover some gems in the world of budget home theater. Our review staff works hard to identify which home theater products are the best for your buck, and products are always evaluated on a rating-per-dollar scale.

CheapHomeTheater.com focuses primarily on speakers and home theater receivers, but we also review televisions, projectors, remote controls, and personal video recorders. The reviews are divided into three categories: Look & Feel, Features, and Performance. Inside each of these three categories, the products are rated on a scale between one and five with an overall score at the end of the review. (See Figure A.1.)

Figure A.1

CheapHomeTheater.com focuses on budget home theater products

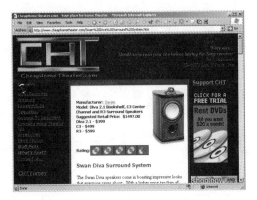

CheapHomeTheater.com also features a forum in which home theater owners—from beginners to advanced—exchange information, opinions, and ideas. The forum is moderated by the CheapHomeTheater.com review staff to ensure quality opinions are posted. The forum also gives readers a place to ask questions and voice opinions about reviews. It's a great place for beginners to acquire knowledge about home theater. (See Figure A.2.)

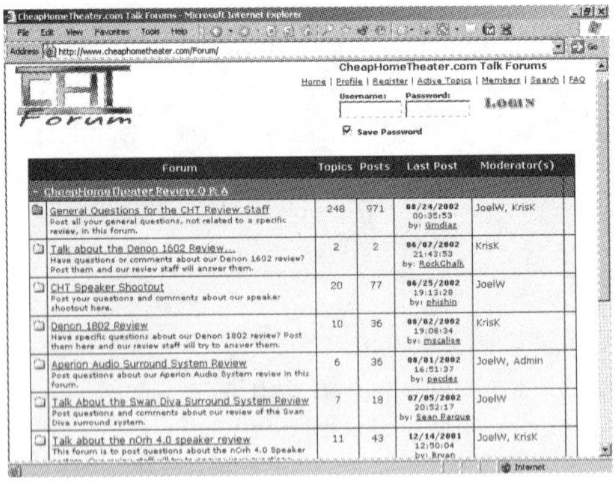

Figure A.2

The CheapHomeTheater.com forum gives readers a chance to interact with the review staff and other home theater enthusiasts

Another favorite section is the Staff Picks, which lets readers know what our review staff has collectively voted on as the best component for the money in several categories. We compare and contrast all these products in a test lab, and publish (online) a list of products we love and highly recommend.

Keohi HDTV

High definition television is coming, but are you ready for it? Keohi HDTV (http://www.keohi.com/keohihdtv/) is the best site for learning about high definition television hardware and programming. However, Keohi HDTV isn't just about high definition television; it also has some great insight on rear projection television sets. Looking for more information about getting your RPTV professionally calibrated or learning how to perform calibrations yourself? Keohi HDTV is a great source for this information.

In fact, many ISF-certified technicians have written detailed material for this site, informing readers how to extract maximum performance from their television set. Do you have a Mitsubishi WS-55805 television but aren't sure how to set the convergence? Brand- and model-specific tips make it easy to find exactly what you are looking for.

Keohi HDTV is also a great site to consult when shopping for a new television. As the manufacturers begin releasing their new television models, the informed ISF technicians examine them and give in-depth reports about the pros and cons. This information is important—use it before you spend thousands of dollars on a big-screen television.

With a name like Keohi HDTV, this site wouldn't be complete without providing an abundance of information on HDTV technology. Keohi HDTV provides quick and easy access about local HDTV setups and satellite broadcasts. There are detailed instructions and tips and tricks for getting your HDTV equipment set up and working properly. (See Figure A.3.)

Figure A.3
Keohi HDTV keeps you in tune with the constantly changing world of HDTV

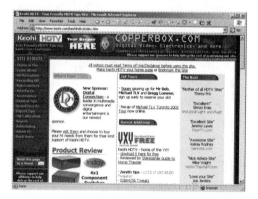

Remote Central

Operating a home theater can be difficult and often requires the use of multiple remotes. Remote Central (http://www.remotecentral.com/) has the biggest collection of detailed reviews of nearly every remote control available. (See Figure A.4.)

Fig A.4
Remote Central is the authority on everything involving remote controls

If you decide to invest in a Philip's Pronto or comparable remote control, you'll certainly want to bookmark Remote Central. Thousands of readers have uploaded files that contain custom layouts and infrared codes for every device you can imagine, and you can download these files for free. These files are a great place for a beginner to start when trying to program a universal remote control.

Remote Central also has a wide variety of forums where you can gain knowledge and trade ideas with other home theater enthusiasts. If you are running into problems programming your remote, chances are someone on the Remote Central message board can point you in the right direction.

Haven't decided on a remote control yet? Remote Central even features the "Clicker Picker," a feature that helps match a user's needs with a suitable remote control. After you've decided on a remote, make sure you check the message boards for the best price (and where to find it).

Forums

Wouldn't you like to ask people who own a certain product their thoughts about it, even after the newness of their purchase has worn off? Well, home theater message boards and forums allow you to do just that and more. You can trade ideas, write reviews, and make quick comments on a wide variety of home theater-related subjects. The Internet features numerous message boards, but the following sections point out a couple of the best.

AVS Forum

AVS Forum (http://www.avsforum.com/) is a great place to explore the video aspects of home theater systems. AVS Forum has a wide variety of message boards for discussions, including some on home theater audio, but the best information on this site is related to projectors, RPTVs, and CRT tube-based televisions. (See Figure A.5.)

Figure A.5
AVS Forum is a great place to talk to others about the benefits and drawbacks of projectors, plasma displays, and RPTVs

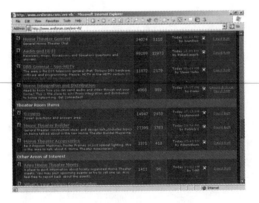

AVS Forum seems to be geared toward intermediate to advanced users, but there are always people willing to help new members. The numerous forum areas may be overwhelming to a new member, so I advise spending some time "lurking" (reading posts without actually posting your own) before jumping into the threads (common name for a conversation on a message board).

Another good area on AVS Forum is the HDTV section. The HDTV areas collect lots of information about local and satellite HDTV developments. There are separate forums dedicated to discussing the pros and cons of specific HDTV hardware, HDTV programming, and the developing HDTV recording forum. The HDTV area is a great place to go to clear up a question you might have about, for example, what is needed to achieve high-definition television in your home.

Digital Theater Forum

Although Digital Theater Forum (http://www.digitaltheater.com/cfb/index.cfm) isn't nearly as well-rounded as AVS Forum or Home Theater Forum (see the following section), it is perhaps the best place to discuss purely home theater audio components (see Figure A.6). If you are curious about separates, home theater receivers, speakers, or subwoofers, this site is for you. Many audiophiles hang out in this forum helping out the less-informed crowd. Digital Theater offers a much smaller number of forums than AVS Forum, but that may make it easier for new members to find what they are looking for.

Figure A.6
Digital Theater Forum isn't as comprehensive as other sites, but it features great information about the audio aspects of home theater

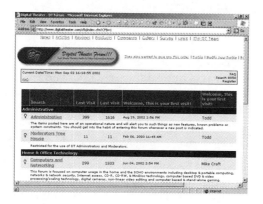

Although they aren't as comprehensive as AVS Forums, the video forums on Digital Theater are decent, especially for beginners. These forums may be easier for a beginner to break into, because they aren't divided into many categories. At Digital Theater, a single Video Components forum exists to talk about everything from DVD players to high-end DLP projectors.

A couple of other notable forums on Digital Theater are the Home Automation and System Integration forums. These forums can help those looking to gain ultimate control over all the devices in their system, and how to make them work well together. These forums help you understand the possibilities for interaction between all the pieces that make up your home theater system.

Home Theater Forum

When I first started in the world of home theater, I spent countless hours reading posts on Home Theater Forum. Even to this day, I spend a good amount of time on Home Theater Forum (http://www.hometheaterforum.com), keeping up with the latest in home theater. A great place for beginners and experts alike, Home Theater Forum is a fine example of a message board that is done right. Home Theater Forum breaks up the forums into categories like Home Theater Basics, Receivers and Separates, and Speakers and Subwoofers. By breaking the huge subject of home theater into small groups, the site makes finding an answer to your particular question easy. (See Figure A.7.)

Figure A.7
Home Theater Forum offers an endless amount of information about everything home theater

If you are just starting out in home theater, jump into the Home Theater Basics forum to learn from other users what to do and, more importantly, what not to do when shopping for and setting up your home theater components. This is a great place to start when you run into a problem setting up home theater components and the instructions just don't make sense. Home Theater Forum does an incredible job of moderating the forums to ensure that posts contain helpful comments and opinions instead of mere shouting matches about which products are the best.

For the more advanced user, there are forums that address the tough, really technical issues. Thinking about building a dedicated theater room? The site even has a forum dedicated to home theater construction. Are you a do-it-yourself type person? There is even a forum that addresses advanced projects, including things like constructing your own speakers. One of my favorite sections is the Tweaking, Connections, and Accessories forum, which helps you find those little touches, such as remote controls, wires, and connectors that make your home theater system look and sound even better. (See Figure A.8.)

Figure A.8
Home Theater Forum offers a wide variety of areas from beginning to advanced levels

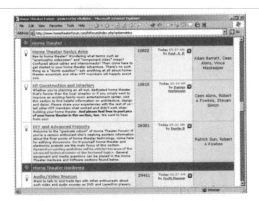

Another great aspect of Home Theater Forum is the classified ads section. Free classified ads allow users to buy and sell home theater equipment. You can find lots of great deals on slightly used equipment here. Finally, there is even a forum where people buy, sell, and trade DVDs.

Manufacturers

If you need detailed, comprehensive information about products, you should go straight to the source: the manufacturer. The manufacturer's website typically offers detailed technical information about products, complete with high-resolution pictures. Although there are far too many manufacturers to list all their websites, the following sections include my picks for the best manufacturer sites in budget home theater. I also mention the features of each site.

This section deals not only with typical mainstream manufacturers (such as Denon, Onkyo, and Sony), but it also goes deeper, showcasing the hidden-bargain-but-high-quality online dealers, such as direct-to-consumer manufacturers Home Theater Direct, Aperion Audio, and Outlaw Audio. These manufacturers are a budget home theater owner's dream, because their products allow you to build a great system without taking out a second mortgage on your house.

Aperion Audio

Aperion Audio's (http://www.aperionaudio.com) website rivals those of the big manufacturers. The thing that most people immediately notice about Aperion Audio's speakers are the great-looking cabinets, in both natural cherry wood and gloss black finishes. This site does a great job explaining what a direct-to-consumer manufacturer is, and the advantages of doing business with one. (See Figure A.9.)

Figure A.9
Aperion Audio's great-looking site also provides helpful information about its products

Aperion Audio not only sells great-sounding speaker packages for 5.1, 6.1, and 7.1 system configurations, but it also packages its speaker systems with popular Onkyo receivers, to create an even greater value for the consumer.

Incredibly detailed, this site has sections devoted to home theater basics and surround sound speaker technology, and there's even a glossary of terms. These sections offer valuable information for you to decide what home theater system is right for you. One more unique aspect Aperion Audio has introduced is financing options that allow you to experience home theater now, while deferring the payment to a later date.

Aperion Audio has done a great job providing copies of independent reviews of their products. These reviews let you see what professional reviewers have to say about the strengths and weaknesses of Aperion Audio products. In addition to professional reviews, customer comments are also on the site, to let you see what customers have to say about their home theater speaker purchases.

Atlantic Technology

Atlantic Technology (http://www.atlantictechnology.com) is a speaker manufacturer that has established a great reputation for providing great-sounding speakers for those on a budget. The Atlantic Technology website features information on various speaker systems, pricing, products reviews, and company information. (See Figure A.10.)

Figure A.10
Atlantic Technology's
website offers some
great features for
helping you get the
most out of your
speaker system

A unique feature of Atlantic Technology's website is an interactive speaker placement tutorial. This feature offers tips to help you set up your speakers for proper placement and application. This interactive guide offers an additional link that provides detailed descriptions of how each speaker in a home theater system can benefit from proper placement. Even if you don't own Atlantic Technology speakers, this is a useful feature.

Atlantic Technology's site also offers detailed specifications on all the speakers within a system. In addition, it also gives you the option of downloading manuals and literature about the speakers. Ready to buy? If so, you'll be able to browse a list of authorized Internet retailers that sell Atlantic Technology speaker packages. Although the site offers a frequently asked questions (FAQ) section, it doesn't have a forum—so if your question can't be answered in the FAQ section, you'll have to go elsewhere.

Axiom Audio

A direct-to-consumer site, Axiom Audio (http://www.axiomaudio.com) has one of the most expansive product lines of all the direct-to-consumer manufacturers. Axiom Audio's website showcases Axiom's products, helps users pick the correct system for their needs, and has useful information to help users connect their system. (See Figure A.11.)

Figure A.11
Axiom Audio's website has a tremendous amount of information about its many products

Axiom Audio's website focuses on giving detailed information to help users determine which Axiom Audio products are best for their particular environment and tastes. The Home Theater Wizard asks a variety of questions to you, the user, including what type of movies and music you prefer, how much you plan to spend, the size of your room, and how powerful your amplifier is. Answer these questions and the Wizard outputs a tailored system that can be added to your shopping cart with a single click. This makes picking a speaker system incredibly simple, even for a new user who isn't sure of all the technical aspects of speaker buying.

Axiom Audio's website also features several different forums, including a home theater forum, a two-channel stereo forum, and an "advice from Axiom owners" forum. These forums are also supplemented by the inclusion of a FAQ section.

Axiom Audio does a great job of providing links to customer and professional reviews as well. The company does this by providing links from each speaker model in its lineup. Simply find the speaker model you are looking for, and click on the link to the customer or professional reviews.

Denon

Denon (http://www.usa.denon.com/) has some of the best home theater receivers on the market, and is right up there with Onkyo (see the "Onkyo" section later in this chapter). Denon has a useful website that provides detailed product information, dealer locations, product updates, and the latest news on all the latest developments with Denon products. (See Figure A.12.)

Figure A.12
Denon's website gives detailed information on some of the best home theater products available

The site has loads of information on Denon's expansive line of home theater receivers, DVD players, speakers, CD players, and Home Theater in a Box solutions. Within the product description pages, Denon includes product photos, detailed specifications sheets, product reviews, and owner's manuals. Denon's site has a links section that points you to additional useful home theater resources on the web, including information on THX certification and the Imaging Science Foundation.

Although Denon's website is thorough, the detailed product information can seem cluttered and difficult to read. If you find yourself having trouble finding detailed specifications on a product, I suggest downloading the electronic product sheets that Denon offers. These product sheets do a great job providing readable product specifications.

Denon is selective about the merchants it sells its products through, because it wants its customers to have a good experience before and after the sale. So, before you bite on that too-good-to-be-true deal on a Denon product from some unknown dealer, consult Denon's website to make sure the retailer has the proper credentials.

Home Theater Direct

Home Theater Direct (http://www.hometheaterdirect.com) was the first direct-to-consumer manufacturer I came across. Although its claims sounded like a late night infomercial, I couldn't help but to test a set of these speakers. I was surprised, shocked even, at the quality of the speakers, especially for the price. I've been one of the biggest supporters of the direct-to-consumer manufacturers since.

Figure A.13
Home Theater Direct is a direct-to-consumer speaker manufacturer; its speakers provide great sound for a low price

Home Theater Direct (HTD) has created a website that showcases and sells its speakers. That means the site also completes sales transactions with customers. Although lacking some of the flash of the big manufacturers, this site provides solid information and details regarding HTD products.

Home Theater Direct has divided its speaker offerings into three levels that reflect quality and price. Within these groupings are links to independent reviews, customer testimonials, and electronic versions of owner's manuals. The website also does a good job detailing the no-risk return policy and the five-year warranty that all of HTD's speakers come with.

I suggest reading the "About Home Theater Direct" section. It goes into great detail explaining the concept behind selling speakers via the Internet, the technology that is in each speaker, and some information on the three groups of speaker systems it sells. Home Theater Direct's website is a great place to start for someone wanting to understand the direct-to-consumer concept.

APPENDIX A

HSU Research

If you ask users of a home theater message board what the best subwoofer under $500 is, I guarantee you at least one person will answer the HSU VTF-2. HSU Research (http://www.hsuresearch.com) has built a reputation for making incredible subwoofers for budget prices. Although the HSU Web page can't compete with the sites from the big manufacturers, it is still a great place to learn about one of the best subwoofers of all time—the VTF-2. (See Figure A.14.)

Figure A.14

HSU Research is home to the famed VTF-2 subwoofer

The main interest point of this website are the reviews of the much heralded VTF-2. Of course, the site also has detailed information on other HSU products. HSU is a direct-to-consumer manufacturer that has established a great reputation for providing quality products at much lower costs than products with similar performance from traditional manufacturers.

If the lack of information on this site leaves you wanting more, I suggest you visit one of the many home theater forums or message boards (mentioned previously). On these forums and message boards, you will find many people who own HSU Research subwoofers and can answer questions for you about these products.

Kenwood

Although Kenwood is known for its car audio systems, it has started to gain popularity in the home theater arena. Kenwood (http://www.kenwoodusa.com) has recently released its high-end Sovereign line of products, and they've been well-received by high-end users. (See Figure A.15.) But Kenwood is not neglecting its budget receivers; they have recently released one of the most affordable THX-certified home theater receivers available in the VR-6070.

Figure A.15
Kenwood's website is full of photos and information about great-sounding home theater gear

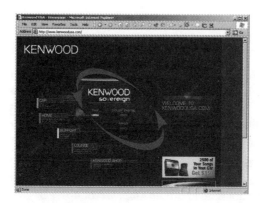

Kenwood has focused on making a great website that provides a wealth of information about its products and common problems incurred when setting up these products. The FAQ and common problems pages can be life-saving if it's late at night and you are struggling to get your home theater operating correctly. Kenwood's website also does a great job explaining technical terms to the lay consumer.

Kenwood has developed a utility on its site that allows users to compare home theater components. This comparison utility works well and allows you to compare two or more products simultaneously.

If Kenwood's website has a shortcoming, it is the lack of detailed photographs. Although the site offers large high-resolution images for the front views of their products, it lacks similar images for the rear views of their products, which would be extremely helpful because rear-view images show the layout of inputs, outputs, and speaker connections.

Klipsch

Klipsch (http://www.klipsch.com) is a well-known speaker and subwoofer manufacturer, mostly because of the horn tweeters in their speakers. Klipsch's is a good-looking website full of information that details its product line. Although Klipsch products can be found in retail stores, Klipsch also has an online store where you can buy products. (See Figure A.16.)

Figure A.16
Klipsch has an expansive website with lots of product information

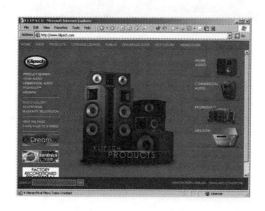

By far, Klipsch has the best collection of product photos on any home theater website. Not only does the site show good, high-resolution images of Klipsch products, it also includes multiple product shots and shows how these products can be incorporated into home theater rooms.

The Listening Lounge section of the website is unique and fun. Inside the Listening Lounge, there is a section that defines common audiophile terminology, and another section that has various Klipsch pictures, which can be downloaded for display as wallpaper on your computer's desktop. Another great feature of the Klipsch site is the Klipsch Advertising section that showcases current and classic Klipsch advertising campaigns.

Klipsch also has a forum where you can discuss the pros and cons of Klipsch products with other enthusiasts. These high-traffic forums are broken into multiple categories, including technical questions, troubleshooting, and home theater inquiries. If you are thinking of purchasing Klipsch speakers, the Klipsch forums are a great place to talk about the different models of speakers and what receiver to team the speakers with.

nOrh

Easily possessing the most distinguishable speaker around, nOrh (http://www.norh.com) loudspeakers are another entry into the direct-to-consumer speaker market. nOrh Loudspeakers have looks that you will either love or hate (see the website image in Figure A.17). Regardless of what you think about the looks, you'll be hard-pressed to find someone who says these speakers don't sound great. nOrh's website helps explain the background behind the unique design of the nOrh speakers.

Figure A.17
The nOrh loudspeakers website has a wide range of information, from history to detailed technical information

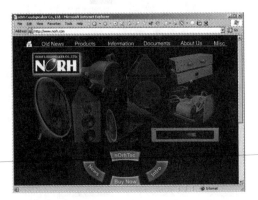

nOrh's website has an in-depth description of the details behind its unconventional speaker cabinet design. The site also has a section devoted to the latest news, keeping readers up-to-date on current happenings. Another great asset to the site is an article that lays out the differences between a system set up for music reproduction and a system built for home theater applications.

Like all direct-to-consumer manufacturers, nOrh's website allows readers to purchase nOrh speakers from the site. Price sheets are abundant, but a good comparison feature isn't currently available. To discern which nOrh speaker is right for you, you'll have to do the digging yourself by looking through their various product lines. This is no small task considering the vast numbers of speakers nOrh lists on its website.

Onkyo

Onkyo (http://www.onkyousa.com) has made a name for itself as a high-end manufacturer whose components offer great features and even better sound. Recently, however, Onkyo has been making waves in the budget home theater market by offering lower-priced components that also include lots of features and great sound that was once only found in components costing hundreds of dollars more. Onkyo manufacturers home theater receivers, DVD players, speaker systems, amplifiers, and other home theater-related gear.(See Figure A.18.)

Figure A.18
Onkyo produces great-performing home theater equipment

Although Onkyo produces many different home theater components, the company is most well-known for its home theater receivers. Onkyo's website offers detailed specifications on its receivers, which makes it easy to decide which receiver is best for you. Great photos of the front and rear of the home theater receivers also offer you a good look at the product—all without leaving your house. (See Figure A.19.)

Figure A.19
Onkyo's website shows detailed information about its receivers and makes comparison shopping easy

A great feature of Onkyo's website is the comparison feature. To use it, first select a receiver model, then choose "compare," and then pick any receiver in Onkyo's lineup to compare it against. Detailed specifications of the two models are listed side-by-side so the differences between the two models are clear. This comparison feature can help you decide if you should upgrade to the next higher-priced model, answering that most important question: Are the added features really worth the extra dollars?

After you've settled on a particular model, you can use the dealer search to find an authorized Onkyo dealer in your area. When buying home theater products, it's important that you buy from an authorized dealer; otherwise, the warranty may not be honored. The Onkyo site also lists authorized Internet dealers if you are interested in buying an Onkyo product via the Internet.

An often overlooked but valuable resource is the ability to download an electronic copy of the owner's manual from the website. For instance, if you are trying to program your remote control to operate the television, but you can't remember how to program it or don't know where your manual is, you can get it from the site for free, right now. The site also provides downloads of Onkyo's latest product brochures.

Outlaw Audio

Spend some time on a home theater message board and it won't be long before you see someone singing the praises of Outlaw Audio. Outlaw Audio (http://www.outlawaudio.com) has some impressive credentials. It built a budget home theater receiver that rivals much more expensive receivers, and some of the company's high-end amplifiers are loved by audiophiles. (See Figure A.20.)

Figure A.20
Outlaw Audio makes both budget and high-end components

Outlaw Audio's website offers detailed information about its small but impressive line of products. Links to independent reviews allow you to read what the professionals say about Outlaw's products. If that isn't enough, you can visit the message board area, dubbed the Outlaw Saloon, and talk to others about Outlaw Audio's products.

Outlaw Audio also provides good information in the form of a frequently asked questions (FAQ) section. This is supplemented with tips, tricks, and additional material that helps you get the most out of your Outlaw Audio product. Both owner's manuals and product sheets are available for download at no charge. In addition, the monthly Outlaw Audio newsletter keeps readers informed on company developments.

Sony

Sony (http://www.sel.sony.com) is perhaps the most recognizable brand name in electronics, with its incredibly wide range of products from audio to video and from budget to high-end. Sony's website showcases its products and helps educate consumers on the details of each product in Sony's expansive lineup.

Sony's website includes some great home theater products, in both the audio and video areas. On the video side, Sony is known for its flat display Wega television sets, which provide the best picture available in a CRT tube-based television. On the audio side, Sony ES has been a big name in high-end receivers and separates for years. Throw into the mix a wide range of speakers, DVD players, CD players, and accessories, and this site may be the only website you need. (See Figure A.21.)

Figure A.21
Sony's website has hundreds of pages full of home theater products of all sorts

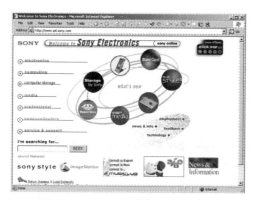

Although Sony's website has an abundance of products, it falls short in features compared to other manufacturers. Sony doesn't provide detailed photos, owner's manuals, or any comparison features (like Denon and Onkyo provide). So, if you are looking for in-depth information on Sony products, the Sony website is a good place to start, but you may find yourself needing more information before being able to make a decision.

SV Subwoofers

SV Subwoofers (http://www.svsubwoofers.com) is a similar phenomenon to HSU Research. SV Subwoofers (SVS) is a direct-to-consumer manufacturer that has established a huge presence in the home theater subwoofer area. The SV Subwoofers website has a collection of product information, reviews, and an online store where you can purchase the products. (See Figure A.22.)

Figure A.22
SV subwoofers are loved on Internet message boards for good reason

SV Subwoofers' website does a great job of providing detailed information that helps you identify the features, size, and type of subwoofer that is right for you. SVS also provides reviews of its products and customer comments. Also available on the website are a series of frequently asked questions, technical help, and information about the company.

Another unique item on SV Subwoofers site is the inclusion of performance charts. These charts show the frequency response of the subwoofers over the usable range, giving you a good indication of how the subwoofers perform in home theater applications. It's touches like this that make you realize SVS is serious about performance.

Yamaha

Yamaha (http://www.yamaha.com) has been a big player in the audio industry for years. Today, it continues to produce top-quality home theater gear. Yamaha's website does a good job organizing a wide range of products into groups that help customers find what they are looking for—quickly. Like Onkyo and Denon, Yamaha has a plethora of information about its products, but Yamaha goes one step further and includes not only owner's manuals, but also hookup diagrams. (See Figure A.23.)

Figure A.23
Yamaha's website is well-organized and provides a wealth of information

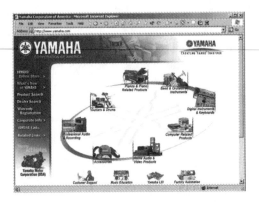

Yamaha's website has numerous other features, including frequently asked questions (FAQ), featured products, comparison charts (see Figure A.24), and a dealer locator. The FAQ page is a great resource for beginners looking for answers to common problems. Couple the FAQ pages with the detailed hookup diagrams that explain the steps needed to establish connections among various devices, and you can see Yamaha has done a great job building a website that provides valuable information to readers.

Figure A.24
Yamaha's website offers comparison charts to highlight feature differences

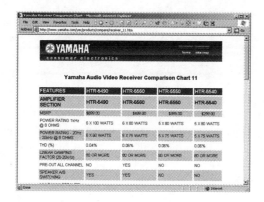

Yamaha provides detailed technical specifications on all its online products, including downloadable owner's manuals and product catalogs. Yamaha also offers a multitude of high-resolution photographs that give you a detailed look at these products. One more feature Yamaha provides is the option to "look inside" some of their products, with cutaway views showing the details inside the components. These high-tech views showcase the attention to detail that Yamaha has taken in producing its components.

Online Retailers

Although a direct-to-consumer manufacturer directly sells its products on its website, if you are looking to buy new products online from traditional manufacturers, you need to look elsewhere. You must go through an authorized web dealer. The websites detailed in the following sections are my picks as the most helpful websites to use when researching and buying components for your home theater system.

Crutchfield

Perhaps the best site around for researching products, Crutchfield (http://www.crutchfield.com) is perfect for those who don't mind paying a little extra for service after the sale. Crutchfield's website is unrivaled in terms of high-resolution, close-up pictures, and detailed information about products. It's one of the easiest websites to navigate, which makes it a perfect place for new shoppers to begin their search. (See Figure A.25.)

Figure A.25
Crutchfield's website is
the best website for
researching audio and
video products

Crutchfield provides a wealth of background information on home theater-related topics and
how-to guides to help you understand what types of products fit your needs. The site also has a
glossary of terms, frequently asked questions, and system-building basics. Free downloads of the
site's how-to guides are also available, so you can have a printed copy when you go shopping or
attempt to hook up your system for the first time.

The real strength of Crutchfield's website is the easy-to-read, but very thorough, product
descriptions, specifications, and photos. If Crutchfield stocks a home theater product, you can
bet it has many high-resolution images that show you every detail of that product. Crutchfield's
product specifications are also easy-to-read and are quite detailed. (See Figure A.26.)

Figure A.26
Crutchfield's detailed
product specifications
are great for getting a
quick understanding of
a product's feature set

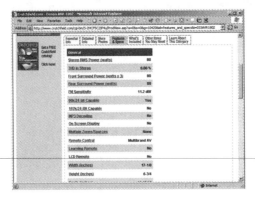

Although Crutchfield doesn't offer any forums to talk to other users, the site does have a
qualified sales staff that recommends products to fit your needs. As mentioned, Crutchfield
service is second to none on service after the sale, so if you are concerned about what happens
when you get the products home, Crutchfield should be your top spot for shopping.

Aside from shopping, Crutchfield's website is a great place to gain an in-depth understanding of
home theater systems. The site has information on everything from building a home theater
room from scratch to figuring out the different surround sound formats to use in your home

theater. The How To Choose guide helps you understand how the various home theater components work together. Crutchfield offers detailed articles on nearly every home theater component and device, so if you aren't clear about a component's function, be sure to check out Crutchfield.

J&R

J&R (http://www.jandr.com) epitomizes an audio and video superstore. It offers an endless number of products via its website. Although the website isn't as easy to navigate or as informative as Crutchfield's, J&R does offer some great prices on some of the best products in home theater. (See Figure A.27.)

Figure A.27
J&R's website can be tough to navigate, but the prices are often worth the search

J&R has a huge selection of products from budget to high-end. These products are grouped into product categories, but can also be found in brand-specific stores, such as the Sony store that showcases only Sony products. J&R also carries all the biggest names in home theater, such as Onkyo, Sony, Panasonic, Harmon Kardon, and Yamaha.

Although J&R does have some basic home theater information on its site, don't expect to find any home theater guides, how-to's, or detailed instructions. J&R is a good website for those who have decided what products to buy and are just in search of the best price. J&R is not a good website for those looking to develop an in-depth understanding of the products or of home theater.

OneCall

I think of OneCall (http://www.onecall.com) as the exact opposite of Crutchfield. Crutchfield has higher prices with a great, easy-to-navigate site, whereas OneCall has better prices but their site leaves a lot to be desired. If you can find the product you are looking for in the maze that is OneCall's website, chances are, it is available for a good price. However, if you don't want to wander around looking for products, you might want to avoid this site. (See Figure A.28.)

APPENDIX A

Figure A.28
OneCall's website offers great prices, but finding items can be a headache

OneCall has a similar product range to Crutchfield and J&R. One notable thing about OneCall is that they do carry the distinction of being an authorized retailer for several quality manufacturers, including Onkyo. This means you can buy Onkyo products from OneCall without having to worry about not getting factory warranty coverage in the event you have a problem with your new product.

OneCall has some unique features that might interest people looking for something different. For instance, they offer Home Theater Package Specials that combine a speaker system and a home theater receiver for a custom-built solution. These solutions are often available for a significant discount compared to buying the products separately.

OneCall is a place where bargain shoppers thrive. If you are willing to go to some extra hassle to save some money, OneCall is the place for you. Those shoppers willing to pay a little more for the added convenience and service should probably stick to shopping at Crutchfield.

Appendix B
Real World Home Theater Examples

This appendix introduces you to real-world examples of different home theater setups. The intent here is to give you ideas for your own home theater room. Although some of the following home theaters don't fall in the under $3,000 category, they still contain great ideas—such as how to hide all your home theater components and what to do when space is limited—that you can borrow and incorporate into your own home theater setup.

As you examine the following examples, notice how several setups have quirky room situations that require the speakers to be placed in a less than optimal setting. Your room might be similar, so take note. Unless you have the luxury of building a dedicated home theater room, you'll most likely have to make some sacrifices in speaker placement as well.

Another thing to keep in mind are the differences in room treatments. Several of the following home theater rooms contain hardwood floors, which have a tendency to reflect sound. You can see what these home theater enthusiasts have done to combat this drawback. Remember that nearly every potential home theater room has something odd about it that makes it less than ideal for home theater, but when you take steps to counter each room's problems, you can still achieve astonishing surround sound and exceptional video performance, as the following folks have done.

Video-Oriented Home Theater Systems

Following are three real-world examples of home theater systems that are primarily slanted toward achieving great-looking video.

Simple but Striking

My friend Jake has assembled a home theater setup that people envy. Although it doesn't showcase the biggest television or contain "separates," the quality of his home theater is tough to match. Jake has taken the approach that bigger isn't always better, that simple works better than overkill. He always keeps a close eye on the tiny details that make his system look and perform incredibly. (See Figure B.1.)

Figure B.1
Jake's home theater is clean-looking, great-sounding, and tweaked with extreme audio and video calibration to get maximum performance from his components

Jake lives in an older house that has hardwood floors and high ceilings. As mentioned, wood flooring can create problems in home theaters because of sound reflection. Home theater enthusiasts describe this type of room as "more alive" than a carpeted room—often too alive. To combat the bouncing sound, Jake uses a big, oversized couch to absorb some of the sound and reduce reflections. (See Figure B.2.) This strategy works.

Figure B.2
An oversized couch provides a good seating area and helps reduce sound reflections

Jake's theater resides in a 12 × 20-foot room, which is rather small for home theater. But the rectangularity of Jake's room is a big plus, because rectangular rooms are preferable to square-shaped rooms, which tend to have problems with signal cancellation (sound waves bouncing off the walls and interfering with each other). Jake's room has several windows along one side wall and directly behind the television monitor. Because rear projection television sets are susceptible to glare, Jake has installed window treatments that allow him to control the amount of light entering the room.

One unusual aspect of Jake's home theater room is an arched doorway on the rear wall that opens to a formal dining area. To the left of the room's rear wall is the house's front entryway. To the right of the rear wall is a hallway that leads to other parts of the house. This hallway is a high-traffic area, because it serves as the entrance to the theater room from both outside and inside the house. (See Figure B.3.)

Figure B.3
The rear of Jake's home theater room opens to another area of the house

A problem that Jake had to overcome was where to place his surround sound speakers. The rear wall of his theater is directly adjacent to his front door, so a bookshelf speaker hanging off the wall wouldn't work. Jake either had to place his speakers to the side of the listening area or find a less intrusive spot on the rear wall. He opted for the latter, as he went with thin, low-profile rear speakers made by Gekko (http://www.gekkoaudio.com/). These speakers extend a little less than two inches from the wall, making minimal impact on the room. (See Figure B.4.) Although Jake loves high-quality home theater sound, he also goes to great lengths to make sure the room still looks uncluttered and homey.

Figure B.4
The Gekko rear speakers provide good sound without making a big impact on the room

In the front of the room, Jake has bookshelf speakers resting on speaker stands. For aesthetic purposes, he has chosen to keep his bookshelf speakers placed slightly behind his television set (instead of the recommended position, which is slightly in front of the television). Jake has also opted to place his center-channel speaker on top of his television. Because he has a large, rear projection television set, the center channel is higher than the optimal position (at ear level). To correct this problem, Jake constructed a brace that raises the rear of the speaker, thus aiming the speaker's sound toward ear level (like most of us, Jake likes to sit on his couch when enjoying his system), as shown in Figure B.5.

Figure B.5
Jake's center channel was aimed too high, so he tilted it down to direct the sound to ear level

Jake is a converted audiophile who used to own a system with "separates"—two separate units, one with a preamplifier and one with a regular amplifier—but he now uses a Sony ES home theater receiver (which has both the preamp and amp in one unit). Jake made the transition from separates to a home theater receiver because the receiver is easier to install, costs less, performs comparably, and is simple to use. Jake's theater also has a Toshiba five-disc DVD progressive scan changer, a Dish Network PVR, a Microsoft Xbox gaming system, and a Samsung HDTV tuner. All these home theater components are housed on an audio rack in the corner of the room. The audio rack has a rear channel to route signal and power cables, which makes the system looks tidy. (See Figure B.6.)

FFigure B.6
Jake has chosen to use an audio rack to organize his equipment

Being the tidy and detail-oriented person he is, Jake does his best to keep his system as visually clean and clutter free as possible. In addition to using the audio rack to manage his many cables, Jake also uses white split-loom tubing—plastic tubing that is split on one side, allowing wires to be concealed inside—to gather the cables that would normally run across the bare floor. Because Jake has white baseboards, the tubing is barely noticeable. Jake has also installed wall plates with modular connection points that allow him to run cable, satellite, speaker, and network wires into two wall plates. (See Figure B.7.)

Figure B.7
Jake's attention to detail is quite evident in his cable management

The latest upgrade to Jake's home theater setup is the subwoofer. Jake recently replaced an expensive NHT subwoofer with a more affordable subwoofer from Aperion Audio. He is quite pleased with the results. He has the subwoofer in a corner, with the driver firing toward the listening area. Because of his hardwood floors, though, Jake had to lower the subwoofer's output level (using the amplifier gain control) to get a really clean, nonvibrating sound. He also put metal spikes on the bottom of the subwoofer to ensure a good solid base with the flooring. And to protect his natural hardwood floors, Jake placed pennies under each of the four spikes. This firmly plants the subwoofer to the floor but keeps it from damaging the finish on the floors—all for only four cents! (See Figure B.8.)

Figure B.8
The subwoofer is corner-loaded but has been adjusted to keep it from overpowering the room

Of course, a great system like this wouldn't be complete without a great television monitor. Jake currently has a Sony 51-inch wide-screen, HD-ready television, and he has gone to great lengths tweaking its convergence to ensure the picture quality is optimal. Moreover, the television originally came with a blue front grill, but to make it match the rest of his theater, Jake recovered the grill with black fabric. These are the small touches that make Jake's home theater room enviable.

A Bigger Budget System

Jennifer and Jason have built a great-looking system that throws the budget out the door in exchange for all-out performance. Featuring THX-certified components and a huge big-screen television, theirs is a system most of us can only dream about. Although Jason had no problem picking top-notch components for his system, getting them to perform well in a room with unconventional form was difficult. (See Figure B.9.)

Figure B.9
Jennifer and Jason's
home theater is a
complex system with
great performance and
simple looks

Most of one side of this home theater room opens into a kitchen, so the room basically has only one sidewall. This configuration makes it impossible to mount speakers on the side of the listening area, leaving only the rear as a mounting option for surround speakers. (See Figure B.10.) The rear wall is an arched doorway that opens into a formal living area. To keep from having the speakers detract from the looks of the room, Jason needed to mount the speakers above eye level. (See Figure B.11.)

Figure B.10
The open room layout
made surround sound
speaker placement
difficult

Jason chose M&K tripole speakers (http://www.mksound.com) for his surround sound. These speakers are a good choice for this application, because they not only have the encompassing sound feature of bipolar speakers, but they also possess the characteristics found in a direct-radiating speaker—a speaker that emits sound toward the area it faces, similar to a bookshelf speaker.

Figure B.11
The rear speaker placement had to be adjusted because of the room's layout

You may have noticed in Figure B.9 that there is no visible component rack in this home theater. That's because Jason has taken the ultimate step in creating a clean-looking home theater system. He put his home theater components in a separate audio closet located in the adjoining hallway. (See Figure B.12.) By putting the components in another area, Jason has little to do to minimize the visual impact of all his cables.

Figure B.12
The separate audio closet allows easy access to home theater components, and it keeps the components and cables out of the way

The audio closet keeps cabling clutter out of sight, but it also creates a problem—remote control signals don't penetrate walls. To work around this problem, Jason opted to use an IR repeater. An IR repeater features a small "eye" that receives the infrared signal from the remote control and transmits the signal through a wire back to the audio closet. The signal is then sent to the proper component and the function is performed. The small "eye" is barely visible, as you can see in Figure B.13.

Figure B.13
The small IR eye on the front of the television sends the remote control commands back to the audio closet

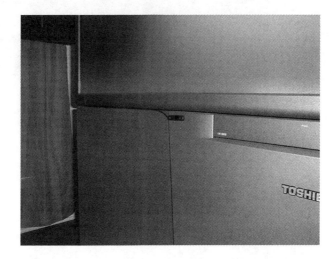

Like Jake's home theater room, Jennifer and Jason's room has hardwood flooring. To combat the reflective tendencies of the flooring, they put a large fabric couch and several chairs in the room. In addition, they placed an area rug on the floor in the middle of the room, which helps to further absorb sound waves.

To match the M&K speakers in the rear of his system, Jason purchased the much-heralded M&K S-150 THX speakers. (See Figure B.14.) Jason also selected an M&K matching center channel to complement his main speakers. He placed these speakers on M&K stands. Although the stands don't offer any cable management channels, Jason uses black zip ties to secure the speaker wire to the back of the stands, keeping the wires out of sight.

Figure B.14
The M&K S-150 THX speakers feel right at home in this high-end system

Keeping with his optimum positioning philosophy, Jason put his front speakers about six inches in front of his television monitor. This aids in realistic sound re-creation, equaling the distance between the front three speakers and the listening area. (See Figure B.15.)

Figure B.15
Positioning the speakers slightly in front of the television helps create a balanced sound field

Tucked neatly in the corner sits an M&K subwoofer. Jason realizes his subwoofer is in a less than optimal position, but to keep the theater looking as good as it sounds, he has no other option. Luckily, the M&K subwoofer is more than capable of filling the room with great sound, even if some of the bass gets lost in the hallway. (See Figure B.16.)

Figure B.16
Jason chose to sacrifice some performance from his subwoofer by placing it in the corner, but such placement puts the subwoofer almost out of sight

To accompany the incredible sound system, Jennifer and Jason's television has a 65-inch wide-screen. This television, combined with the superb audio system, creates an awesome home theater experience.

This home theater room has several windows that initially created a serious glare problem (on the television screen). To solve this problem, Jennifer installed shutters and window treatments. (See Figure B.17.) Now they, not the sun, control how much light enters the room.

Figure B.17
To keep out unwanted light and minimize glare on their large television set, Jennifer installed shutters

As you can see, despite several layout problems, Jennifer and Jason have created a tremendous-looking home theater system. Although theirs can't be classified as a "budget" system, it does contain some great ideas that you can incorporate into your system. Don't let an unusual room layout deter you from creating a great-sounding and visually-appealing home theater, as all home theaters owners have to deal with less-than-ideal conditions.

Solarc Inc.'s Home Theater

How do you build a home theater room that also doubles as a lunchroom for 100 employees? With a lot of planning, that's how. Solarc, a software company in Tulsa, decided to build a home theater room as an added perk for its employees. By doing so, the company had the complicated task of designing a room that would have a great home theater sound but would be durable enough to double as the employee lunchroom. (See Figure B.18.)

Figure B.18
The Solarc home theater room had to be both functional and durable

The first stage of the Solarc home theater room involved designing a way to keep the audio and video equipment out of the way of all the daily traffic. This was accomplished by building a closet with a wall-opening for the television monitor and a built-in component rack. The closet allows storage and easy access to wiring while keeping the expensive home theater equipment out of the way. The front and center channel speakers are recessed into the wall to ensure they stay out of the way as well. (See Figure B.19.)

Figure B.19
The recessed television and speakers keep the home theater equipment safely out of the way

The Solarc home theater system uses five identical NHT speakers. This is a great setup that allows you to get the same tonal equality for all speakers, because they all use the same drivers. A Marantz home theater receiver, a Sony VCR, and a Pioneer DVD player are also part of the system. An NHT subwoofer is recessed in the lower-left side of the theater and is covered by a mesh fabric grill. (See Figure B.20.) The television set is a Pioneer Elite.

Figure B.20
Even the NHT subwoofer is hidden from view in the Solarc home theater

Because it wasn't possible to recess the rear speakers in the wall, Solar opted to mount them on the wall, just over 6.5 feet off the floor. This enables all but extremely tall people to walk under the speakers without hitting them. (See Figure B.21.) Although this height is less than optimal (it's a little high), the conditions warranted it, and the speakers still sound great.

Figure B.21
The NHT surround speakers were mounted high so people could walk below them

The most innovative aspect of Solarc's home theater room is the seating arrangements. Solarc wanted a completely flexible seating arrangement that would accommodate the wide variety of uses for this multi-purpose room. This was accomplished by using small, portable chairs.

Audio-Oriented Home Theater Systems

Following are two real-world examples of home theater systems that are primarily slanted toward achieving great-sounding video.

Great Sound, Great Looks

Bryan and Cindy are a typical couple. Bryan wanted a great home theater setup and Cindy wanted a gorgeous armoire. They each got what they wanted, and the result is a functional home theater that doesn't detract from Cindy's perfectly decorated home. Their home theater is proof that you can have the best of both worlds, a home theater system that both sounds and looks great. (See Figure B.22.)

Figure B.22
Bryan and Cindy's home theater components are contained in a gorgeous wood armoire

The first step in creating a home theater system that both Cindy and Bryan could agree on was purchasing an armoire that would dictate the size of their television-to-be. After measuring the armoire they wanted, they realized they could fit a 32-inch television it in. After purchasing the armoire, they modified the back of it slightly and placed their new 32-inch Sony Wega XBR inside. The Sony television provides the best possible picture in a CRT tube-based television and is a good fit for their available monitor space. (See Figure B.23.)

Figure B.23
The Sony Wega
television fits snuggly
inside the armoire, and
provides great video

The armoire not only holds the television set, but it also houses the other home theater components. This home theater consists of a Sony ES home theater receiver, a Dish Network PVR, a Replay PVR, a Toshiba DVD player, a Microsoft Xbox, a Sony PlayStation2, and a Nintendo GameCube. The wires are all nicely concealed in the armoire, despite the large number of them needed to connect all these devices. (See Figure B.24.) One disadvantage to this setup, though, is that access to the rear panels of these components is limited. This can make upgrades and alterations time-consuming.

An additional concern of this setup is heat buildup from the home theater equipment. Home theater receivers get hot quickly and can overheat if not ventilated properly. With this in mind, Bryan keeps the Sony receiver on the lowest shelf in the armoire. He also makes sure that no other component rests on top of the receiver.

Figure B.24
The armoire houses all
the home theater
components and keeps
the wires out of sight
and out of mind

They opted to neatly place the powered subwoofer directly to the side of the armoire. When the doors of the armoire are open, the subwoofer (a Sony SA-WM40) is barely visible. (See Figure B.25.) Placing the subwoofer in close proximity to the receiver also helps minimize cable length.

Figure B.25
The Sony powered subwoofer is almost concealed in its placement to the side of the armoire

Bryan and Cindy's house has several quirks that make their home theater setup unique. First, as in Jennifer and Jason's house, the designated home theater room lacks a full side wall, because one wall is an entrance to the kitchen area. Second, the room features a high, cathedral-style ceiling. Finally, like Jake's home theater, theirs has wood flooring.

With no right side wall, rear speaker placement became an issue, because Bryan couldn't mount a speaker. Thus, he was forced to do one of two things: use a bookshelf stand placed to the side of the listening area or mount the speakers on the rear wall. Bryan chose the latter, mounting the speakers quite high—over six feet above ear level—on the rear wall. (See Figure B.26.) He knew this was high, so he wisely aimed the speakers downward toward the listening area. (See Figure B.27.) In addition to properly aiming the speakers, Bryan used a calibration disc in combination with a decibel meter to boost the speaker levels of the rear surrounds to obtain the same output levels as the main front speakers. Another smart move Bryan made was that instead of going with typical bookshelf speakers, he purchased a set of tripole speakers from M&K Sound (http://www.mksound.com). These tripole speakers are a hybrid of a direct-radiating speaker and a bipolar speaker, and their small size makes them unobtrusive.

Figure B.26
The M&K tripole speakers are mounted behind the listening area, high on the wall to keep the visual impact to a minimum

Figure B.27
The small rear speakers have been professionally wired through the ceiling and are pointed toward the listening area

After the armoire was filled with all the home theater components and television, Bryan realized there wasn't sufficient space for the center channel to reside inside the armoire. Faced with few options, Bryan decided to place the center channel speaker on top of the armoire, over six feet above ear level. Much as Jake did with his center channel, Bryan elevated the rear of the center channel to aim the drivers in the speaker toward the listening area. (See Figure B.28.) Although this isn't an ideal setup, Bryan makes it work; the center channel sounds great.

Figure B.28
Because of the height of his center channel, Bryan opted to tilt the speaker to direct the sound toward the listening area

As strange as it seems, rooms with unusual geometry are actually some of the best places to build a home theater system. The varied geometry can alleviate the problem of sound waves reflecting off the walls and interfering with other sound waves. In Bryan and Cindy's home theater room, the high ceilings actually help the sound. However, the hardwood floors tend to make the room a bit echoic, so they countered this by putting a large chair and a sofa in the listening area. These room treatments help Bryan achieve the sound he wants and enable Cindy to have sitting room for her guests when she's entertaining.

Bryan completed his home theater setup by purchasing front left and right Level III bookshelf speakers from Home Theater Direct—with a timbre matched Level III center channel. (See Figure B.29.) Bryan chose to purchase stands from Home Theater Direct, to have the speakers placed at ear level. The stands feature cable management, keeping the speaker wires out of sight.

Figure B.29
The Home Theater Direct Level III speakers provide big sound for this home theater system

Home Theater System in an Apartment

Like the other owners profiled in this appendix, my friend Anup had room layout problems when setting up his home theater system. But he faced another, more complicated challenge: neighbors. Anup lives in an apartment and has neighbors in the apartments to his left, right, and directly above him. This creates an interesting dilemma: How does Anup experience big theater sound while not upsetting his neighbors? (See Figure B.30.)

Figure B.30
Anup faced the difficult task of building a great-sounding home theater system in an apartment

Anup first decided to buy floor-standing speakers with good bass output (instead of purchasing a separately powered subwoofer). He did this because bass frequencies travel through walls all too well, so a powered subwoofer would be tough to integrate into a home theater system in an apartment. Anup decided on a pair of Klipsch RF-3 II tower speakers. Each tower possesses two 8-inch drivers to create more than enough bass output for his apartment. (See Figure B.31.)

By opting for tower speakers (not bookshelf speakers), Anup saved himself the added cost of buying stands. Stands start at around $50 and can cost over $100, so purchasing tower speakers wasn't as costly of an upgrade as he initially thought. Because he was saving money by not purchasing the powered subwoofer, the tower speakers were the perfect solution.

Figure B.31
The Klipsch RF-3 II
tower speakers offer
more than enough bass
response for an
apartment

To match the timbre of his Klipsch tower speakers, Anup decided to buy the matching Klipsch center channel. The RC-3 II center channel (see Figure B.32) rests on top of a 32-inch Sony Wega television and offers dual 6.5-inch woofers, making it, too, very capable of good bass response. The great advantage of this system is that if Anup feels he needs more bass at some point in the future, he can easily add a powered subwoofer.

Figure B.32
The big RC-3 II center
channel is a capable
performer

Because Anup's living room is more compact than the typical living room, rear speaker placement was difficult, especially because Anup doesn't have the option of permanently mounting speakers to the rear wall—landlords don't like such things! To solve this problem, Anup bought a pair of Home Theater Direct Level III bookshelf speakers for their forward presentation, which is similar to the presentation of his Klipsch speakers. (See Figure B.33.) Timbre-matching the front speakers is crucial. Matching the front speakers to the rear speakers is recommended but isn't essential, because front-to-rear transitions are less common than left-to-right transitions.

Figure B.33
The Home Theater
Direct Level III speakers
are a good choice for
those looking for low-
cost bookshelf speakers
that can also serve as
surround sound
speakers

As you can see in Figure B.33, the rear speakers are placed on the sides of the sitting area, facing forward instead of aiming toward the listeners. Anup decided not to aim the rear speakers toward the sofa in order to keep the sound from overpowering the listeners.

Anup chose a Denon receiver to go with his Pioneer DVD player and Motorola digital cable receiver. These components rest on a component rack that sits directly to the side of the television system. The audio rack provides a rear cable management channel that allows signal and power cables to be hidden from view.

The aspect of Anup's theater that I really appreciate is that he can upgrade this system in several ways. Anup has started with a system that is more heavily weighted on the audio aspect than the video aspect. However, when space and budget allow, he is only a big screen away from an ultimate system. The system also leaves areas for improvement on the audio side, in which case he'll opt to add a powered subwoofer or upgrade his home theater receiver, both of which can be done without much complication.

As you can see in the previous examples, picking high-quality components isn't all that's required for a great home theater system. You also need to know how to set up and position your components to get the best possible home theater experience from your equipment and your home theater room. The underlying point in all these examples is that small treatments and adjustments can often make a potentially frustrating home theater system a most enjoyable one. Good luck on yours!

Appendix C
Glossary

A

AC-3
A name originally given to the surround sound format now known as Dolby Digital.

A/V
The abbreviation for Audio/Video.

Amplifier
A device that takes an input signal from another device, such as a DVD player or VCR, and reproduces it at a higher volume level. An amplifier can either be a stand-alone unit or, more commonly, integrated inside a home theater receiver.

Anamorphic Wide-screen
A term used to describe the process of squeezing a wide-screen image onto a standard 1.33:1 (4x3) aspect ratio DVD, and then stretched back out during playback. The result is increased picture resolution and less wasted resolution on the black bars. Anamorphic images are best when viewed on a wide-screen (16x9) television monitor because these displays stretch the image back to its original width. Displaying these images on a standard 1.33:1 aspect ratio television (4x3) requires the image to be stretched vertically by the DVD player, thus decreasing resolution. DVD players are equipped with setup options that allow the selection of a 4x3 or 16x9 aspect ratio television set.

Aspect Ratio
A value given to the ratio of the width to the height of a television monitor. A wide-screen television has an aspect ratio of 1.78:1. This aspect ratio is also often referred to as 16x9. A standard definition, nonwide-screen television has an aspect ratio of 1.33:1. This aspect ratio is often referred to as 4x3.

Audiophile

A person very concerned with the quality of sound. Audiophiles usually spend large sums of money to ensure they are getting the absolute best sound reproduction possible.

Average Picture Level (APL)

The percentage of the picture level on a scale between the level of black and white. The APL is a factor when performing video calibrations. A high APL is a very bright image that has a high concentration of white; a low APL is a dark, primarily black, image.

B

Banana Plug

A speaker connection that is thicker in the middle of the shaft than the ends, and is inserted into a binding post to establish a connection to a speaker or amplifier. (See Figure G.1.)

Figure G.1
Banana plugs are a great way to establish connections on speakers and receivers

Bass Extension

The lowest frequency a speaker will produce. For example, a bookshelf speaker's bass extension could be 56 Hz, whereas a powered subwoofer's bass extension might be 22 Hz.

Big Screen

A generic term given to television sets with a diagonal length measuring at least 36 inches. (See Figure G.2.)

Figure G.2
Big screen televisions have been synonymous with home theater systems

Bipolar Speaker

A speaker that outputs sound in two directions by using two speakers working in phase together. Bipolar speakers offer a wide dispersion pattern compared to bookshelf speakers, but typically suffer in re-creating subtle sounds. Bipolar speakers are typically used as rear speakers in a home theater system, and are often mounted above ear level to the side of the listening area. (See Figure G.3.)

Figure G.3
Bipolar speakers use two separate driver sets firing in different directions to create an enveloping sound

Bi-amping

The process of using two separate amplifiers to power a single speaker. One amplifier is used to drive the tweeter (high frequencies) and the other is used to drive the woofer (mid-range and bass frequencies).

Bi-wiring

The process of running two separate sets of speaker wire from a single amplifier to a speaker. One set of speaker wire is connected to the connection point for the high-frequency driver (tweeter). The other set of speaker wire is connected to the connection point for the low-frequency driver (woofer). The theory behind bi-wiring is that the low, bass frequencies demand too much current during intense bass, leading to overall degradation in high-frequency sound reproduction. (See Figure G.4.)

Figure G.4
Bi-wiring uses two sets of speaker wires from the receiver to the speaker to ensure maximum signal quality

APPENDIX C

Binding Posts

A high-quality connection point used on speakers and amplifiers. Binding posts can use a variety of wire terminations, such as bare wire, spades, banana plugs, and banana pins. Binding posts are often dubbed 5-way binding posts, referring to five separate connection types that can be used with these connection points. Binding posts are the preferred connection type for your speakers and amplifiers. (See Figure G.5.)

Figure G.5
Gold-plated binding posts are desired on speakers to ensure the best connections possible

Bookshelf Speaker

A small speaker, usually between 14 and 26 inches in height, that is typically placed on a bookshelf or on a stand to bring the speaker to ear level. Bookshelf speakers can be used for front, rear, and center speakers in a home theater system. A typical bookshelf system has a woofer that is between 4 and 6.5 inches in diameter and a tweeter that handles the high frequencies. Bookshelf speakers are a favorite in budget home theater systems. (See Figure G.6.)

Figure G.6
Bookshelf speakers are the most common speaker type in a budget home theater system

Brightness

The level of black in a video signal. This setting is used in conjunction with contrast to achieve an optimal balance providing black colors that appear black while still providing detail in dark areas.

Burn In

A condition in which stagnant images cause damage to the television screen. The damage is usually an outline of the image that was displayed for a long period of time. High brightness settings can expedite this process due to the intensity of the signal being displayed.

C

Calibration Disc

A DVD disc that is used to obtain optimal audio and video settings from your home theater components. These discs include measured test signals that, when measured with a decibel meter, allow users to ensure that equal volume levels are being output by all of the speakers in a home theater system regardless of acoustical differences in the room. These discs also help optimize video settings on the television monitor to ensure proper brightness, tint, and color settings. The most popular calibration discs are Avia Guide to Home Theater and Video Essentials. (See Figure G.7.)

Figure G.7
Calibration discs are essential in gaining maximum performance from your home theater audio and video system

Center Channel

A speaker that is used to reproduce dialogue and sounds occurring in the middle of the scene. The center channel receives very high usage in DVD movie playback. The center channel should be timbre matched with the left and right speakers so the transition between these speakers cannot be detected. Dolby Digital, DTS, and Dolby Pro Logic I & II use a front-center channel. Dolby Digital EX and DTS ES surround sound formats use a front-center and a rear-center channel. (See Figure G.8.)

Figure G.8
Center-channel speakers are responsible for reproducing the dialogue in DVD movie reproduction

Clipping

A term referring to distortion caused when a speaker or amplifier is operating at a level above its capabilities. This condition usually occurs when the amplifier is being used at a level that is too high.

Coaxial Cable

The type of cable typically used for cable and digital satellite television transmission. Different grades of coaxial cable are available, with the most common being RG-59 and RG-6. RG-6 provides increased shielding and picture quality and is used for digital satellite systems.

Component Video

A video signal connection that separates the video signal into three separate signals. Black and white information is separated from the color information, much like S-Video, but it also separates the color signals. Component video connections offer the best quality video reproduction and should be used if possible. Component video connections are necessary to get progressive scan video output from a DVD player or a high-definition television receiver. (See Figure G.9.)

Figure G.9
Component video is the best video connection method

Composite Video

A video signal connection that uses a single cable to transmit a video signal combining color and black and white information into a single signal. Composite video connections are the basic, lowest quality connections that are commonly used and should be avoided if possible.

Contrast

The level of white in a video picture. This setting works in conjunction with the brightness control to obtain optimum settings at which the picture accurately displays both black and white. High contrast results in an image that is predominately white; low contrast means an image is mainly black.

Convergence

The alignment of the three color guns in a rear projection television set at various points across the screen. Proper convergence is essential to obtaining a high-quality picture from a RPTV. A convergence grid is displayed on the television consisting of horizontal and vertical lines. The intersection points of these lines are adjusted to ensure the red, green, and blue color guns are properly aligned. Another important aspect is to ensure these lines are straight. (See Figure G.10.)

Figure G.10
A convergence grid shows how well the red, green, and blue color guns are aligned at various points on the video display screen

Crossover

A device that routes a certain range of audio signals to a particular component of a speaker. Typically, a crossover routes low, bass frequencies to the woofer and sends high, treble frequencies to the tweeter. Home theater receivers also feature crossovers that send low frequencies to the dedicated subwoofer while routing the high signals, typically those above 80 Hz, to the full-range speakers in the audio system.

CRT Tube-based Television

A television monitor that uses a glass tube with electron guns to project an image. CRT tube-based televisions are the most common television sets. They range in size from 13 inches in diameter to 40 inches in diagonal length. (See Figure G.11.)

Figure G.11
Almost every home has at least one CRT tube-based television set

D

Decibel Meter

A device that measures sound pressure level (SPL). This measure tells the user how loudly an audio signal is being reproduced. Decibel meters are typically used in conjunction with a calibration disc to measure the output level of each speaker in a home theater system to ensure that each speaker outputs the same volume level during playback.

Digital Input

An input on a home theater receiver that receives a digital signal from either an optical cable or a digital coaxial cable. Dolby Digital and DTS surround formats use digital inputs to pass their digital bitstreams to the receiver for the receiver to decode. (See Figure G.12.)

Figure G.12
Digital inputs are required for a receiver to input a Dolby Digital bitstream

Digital Light Processing (DLP)

A video processing method that uses thousands of tiny mirrors pivoting to reflect, or not reflect, colored lights. This technology is used in high-end projectors and television monitors to provide increased picture quality.

Digital Signal Processing

The process of altering a signal in a digital form. Digital signal processing offers advantages over analog signal processing, including the ability to more easily reproduce the alteration.

Digital Television (DTV)

The television programming transmitted in a digital format. High definition television (HDTV) is a high-quality form of digital television.

Dipolar Speaker

A speaker that utilizes drivers on opposite sides of the enclosure with the speakers firing in opposite directions. Unlike bipolar speakers, dipole drivers operate out of phase from the drivers on the opposite side. Dipolar speakers output little to no sound to the side of the speaker, but dipolar speakers offer a very wide dispersion pattern and create an enveloping sound. Dipolar speakers are mainly used as rear speakers.

Direct Broadcast Satellite (DBS)

The digital television programming received by using a small dish and a satellite receiver that decodes the digital signal. DBS systems provide digital audio and video and can offer an increase in picture quality over standard cable television. The two major providers of this service are DirecTV and Dish Network.

Direct Radiating

A speaker that emits sound from the front of the speaker. A bookshelf speaker is an example of a direct-radiating speaker. Bipolar and dipolar speakers are not direct-radiating speakers because they emit sound to the sides of the speaker. (See Figure G.13.)

Figure G.13
Direct-radiating speakers are used for front, center, and rear speaker applications

Direct to the Consumer (DTC)

A manufacturer that sells products directly to the consumer, typically via the Internet. These products are not found at local electronics stores, but offer increased values due to the low overhead associated with selling the products via the Internet as opposed to retail stores. These manufacturers typically offer free trial periods so that consumers can evaluate the products risk-free in their own homes.

APPENDIX C

Direct View

A term used to describe a conventional CRT tube-based television set.

Discrete

An independent source that is completely separated from other sources. For example, Dolby Digital has 5.1 discrete audio channels that are completely separated from each other.

Dispersion

The spreading of sound across an area by a speaker. A speaker that spreads its audio signal over a wide range is said to have a wide dispersion pattern.

Dolby Digital

A discrete, digital surround sound format that uses five full-range speakers and a dedicated low-frequency subwoofer. Dolby Digital is used on DVD discs and HDTV. The sounds are output to front-right, front-center, front-right, rear-left, and rear-right speakers. Dolby Digital is also called "5.1," a reference to the five full-range channels and the dedicated low-frequency effects channel.

Dolby Digital EX

A discrete, digital surround sound format that uses six full-range speakers and a dedicated low-frequency subwoofer channel. In addition to using all the channels present in Dolby Digital, Dolby Digital EX adds a rear-center channel that is created from information from the left and right rear surround channels. This format is also referred to as 6.1 and THX EX.

Dolby Pro Logic (DPL)

A surround sound format that outputs four distinct channels of sound. These four channels are front-right, center, front-left, and rear. The center channel in Dolby Pro Logic is matrixed from the left and right front channels. This means the center channel is a signal created by using information from two other channels. Although Dolby Pro Logic uses two speakers in the rear, the rear audio channel is mono, meaning the two rear speakers play the exact same signal. Dolby Pro Logic also lacks the dedicated low-frequency effects channel present in Dolby Digital. The center and rear channels of Dolby Pro Logic signals also feature a limited frequency reproduction.

Dolby Pro Logic II (DPL II)

An update to the Dolby Pro Logic format that improves on the existing surround sound format. Improvements include the inclusion of a dedicated low-frequency effect channel, stereo rear surround speakers, and an increase in frequency reproduction. Dolby Pro Logic II is backwards compatible with existing Dolby Pro Logic media. This format can give old Dolby Pro Logic material new life by increasing the overall sound quality.

Driver

An individual component of a speaker system, such as a woofer, mid-range, or tweeter.

DTS

Like Dolby Digital, a 5.1 discrete surround sound format that uses five full-range channels and a dedicated low-frequency effects channel. DTS uses different compression and coding methods that are not compatible with Dolby Digital. DTS uses a lower compression ratio than Dolby Digital, which can lead to an increase in sound quality. DTS playback is available on select DVD discs, but also requires a DVD player and a receiver that are DTS capable.

DTS ES

A discrete, digital surround sound format that uses six full-range channels and a dedicated low-frequency effects channel. Two forms of DTS ES are available, DTS ES Matrix and DTS ES Discrete 6.1. DTS ES Matrix uses information from the left and right surround channels to create a rear-center channel, whereas DTS ES Discrete 6.1 actually has center channel information encoded into the disc.

Digital Versatile Disc (DVD)

The standard media for home theater systems. DVDs provide digital audio and video that results in increased picture quality over other media, such as VHS. These discs are the same size as a typical audio compact disc, but they provide a much larger amount of storage space.

DVD-Audio

A surround sound audio format that uses DVD discs to provide increased quality, increased playback length, and full surround sound. These discs can also carry video, but are primarily designed to offer increased quality in audio playback by providing an increased audio bit rate over standard DVD discs. DVD-Audio uses a lossless compression method, unlike standard DVD video discs, which use a lossy compression method.

E

Efficiency

A measure of volume output, rated in decibels, that a speaker produces when given 1 watt of power. Efficiency is a synonym for sensitivity rating.

F

Flat Response

The ability of a speaker to output equal volume levels of a signal over the entire audible range. Many speakers cannot reproduce sounds below 80 Hz at the same level at which they reproduce higher frequencies. A desirable output level curve would show flat response for 80Hz–20 kHz with the subwoofer handling the task of re-creating sounds below 80 Hz. A typical speaker may be rated as 56 Hz–20 kHz (+/- 3 db). The +/- 3 db rating refers to the speaker outputting a response that fluctuates by no more than 3 db over the frequency range stated.

Frequency Range

A range, measured in Hz, in which a device can output a signal without distortion and without significant output gain or loss.

Frequency Response

The frequency range over which a component can output a usable, nondistorted signal. An example of a frequency range rating for a receiver is 20 Hz–20 kHz. An example of a bookshelf speaker's frequency range is 56 Hz–20 kHz. A subwoofer has a more limited frequency response, for example 22 Hz–180 Hz.

Front Projection Display

A video setup that uses a separate projector unit that outputs a video image onto a screen. Movie theaters are a common application that use front projection display technology. Front projection displays are also common in high-end home theater applications. Front projection systems can output a video image over 100 inches in diagonal length.

H

High Definition Television (HDTV)

A digital television signal that uses increased video resolution to provide a more realistic picture. HDTV signals also use Dolby Digital surround sound to obtain pure digital sound. 1080i is the most common HDTV signal. 720p is another comparable signal. HDTV uses a wide-screen aspect ratio of 16x9 (1.78:1).

Home Theater or Home Theater System

A term describing a theater-like experience in the home by the use of a video and surround sound. A typical home theater system consists of a television monitor, DVD player, home theater receiver, and a speaker system. Some home theaters also use a VCR, DBS satellite system, or an HDTV tuner.

I

Imaging

A term that describes how well a signal that is output from a component conveys a sense of depth, width, and placement. An example of good imaging is when you listen to a selection and you can visualize where different sounds from the source were located when the sound was recorded.

Imaging Science Foundation (ISF)

A collection of trained individuals who are certified in calibrating television monitors to obtain the maximum picture quality possible. ISF-trained technicians typically travel around the country and perform calibrations in the customer's home. ISF technicians perform advanced maneuvers that typical users should not try by themselves.

Interconnect

A cable, typically a composite cable, that connects two components in a home theater system. For example, an interconnect conveys an audio signal between a VCR and a home theater receiver. (See Figure G.14.)

Figure G.14
Interconnects are used to transmit audio or video signals between devices in a home theater system

Interlaced Scan

A video display method in which half the lines that make up an image are drawn in a single pass, then the other half of the lines are drawn in a separate, second pass. Standard television programming uses interlaced scan technology. Standard television is often referred to as a 480i signal, referring to the 480 lines of interlaced scan picture that makes up the video image.

L

Laserdisc

A media format that preceded DVD discs and provided Dolby Digital surround sound and high-quality video output. Laserdiscs are 12 inches in diameter. Although the format offered improved-quality audio and video over VCR tapes, the format failed to gain the widespread acceptance that DVD discs have.

Learning Ability

The ability for a universal remote control to learn an infrared code into its internal memory, then be able to reproduce the infrared signal.

Letterbox

A format for showing an image wider than the standard 4x3 aspect ratio of a television accomplished by fitting the picture into the width of the display screen, then using black bars above and below the image. Letterbox formats ensure you see the entire picture, unlike pan and scan formats. (See Figure G.15.)

Figure G.15
Letterbox display allows
the viewing of a source
image that is wider than
the monitor's display

Lossless Compression

A form of compression in which no information is lost when the data is uncompressed. Lossless compression methods are the favorite of audio purists who insist that the original source signals should never be altered. Lossless compression methods can provide a better overall sound, but they require much more storage space than a lossy compression method.

Lossy Compression

A form of compression in which some information from the original source signal is discarded and cannot be recovered. MP3 audio files are a good example of a lossy compression method.

Low Frequency Effect (LFE)

A discrete channel found in Dolby Digital, DTS, and Dolby Pro Logic II formats that carries only low-frequency (below 80 Hz) information. Because this channel is a limited bandwidth channel, it is referred to as the ".1" in a 5.1 surround sound format.

Lumens

The measure of light output from a video source. Projectors are rated in lumens.

M

Macro Commands

A series of commonly used commands that are recorded then executed with the press of a macro button. Common use of macro commands is to turn all the components in a home theater system on or off.

Manufacturers Suggested Retail Price (MSRP)

The price for which the manufacturer suggests a product be sold at retail stores. This is often the price at which large chain electronics stores sell the products; however, you can often find retailers that will sell at prices lower than MSRP.

Mono or Monaural

A recording with only one channel of sound.

Monopole

A synonym for a direct-radiating speaker.

MP3

A type of compression commonly used to reduce the amount of space needed to store audio files. MP3 uses a lossy compression method that discards some of the original signal in order to save space required to store the file.

P

Pan and Scan

A method of cropping an image that is wider than a standard aspect ratio television to fit in the standard aspect ratio size. Pan and scan results in an image that fills the entire screen (without black bars on top and bottom like letterboxing), but it discards the sides of the image.

Passive Subwoofer

A subwoofer that requires the use of an external amplifier, unlike a powered subwoofer, which has an onboard amplifier.

Personal Television Recorder (PTV)

A device that records and plays back television programming onto a hard drive such as those found in personal computers. These devices offer many hours of storage and allow users to time shift programming by pausing live television programming. PTV boxes incorporate software that allows for advanced recording options that VCRs cannot duplicate. Tivo, Replay, and UltimateTV are the three most common PTV brands.

Phase

An expression of how far through the complete cycle a sound wave is. Phase is measured in degrees, with 360 degrees comprising a complete phase cycle. Two waves that are in phase have peaks that coincide. Two waves that are out of phase have peaks that do not coincide. Phase is important because two waves that are 180 degrees out of phase from each other have a cancellation effect, leading to reduced output.

Plasma Television Sets

A display technology that allows television monitors to display crisp pictures while minimizing size. Unlike conventional CRT tube-based television sets, plasma television sets are not deep and can be mounted on the wall.

Ported Enclosure

A type of speaker enclosure that features port tubes that allows the sound and air from the inside of the enclosure to be heard. Ported enclosures are typically louder than sealed enclosures, but can be less accurate than sealed enclosures in re-creating sounds. Ports can be in various locations of the enclosure including the front, rear, and bottom. (See Figure G.16.)

Figure G.16
Ported enclosures are more efficient than sealed enclosures, but can be less accurate

Power

A term used in describing home theater receivers and amplifiers that describes the total amount of output, measured in watts, that the device is capable of producing. For example, a home theater receiver could be described as having 500 watts of power, or 100 watts of power into five channels.

Preamp or Preamplifier

A device commonly found in high-end separates systems that receives, decodes, and switches signals, and then outputs the signal to an external amplification component.

Preprogrammed Codes

A set of predetermined infrared commands in a universal remote control. These codes allow users to set up the remote control to operate a wide variety of devices.

Progressive Scan

A display method in which every line of an image is drawn in a single pass. Computer monitors use progressive scan output to display images. Progressive scan DVD players output a progressive scan image consisting of 480 lines of resolution, often denoted 480p. One of the two major HDTV formats is 720p, a progressive scan image consisting of 720 lines of resolution.

R

RCA Cable or RCA Connector

The term given to a standard, composite cable that features a metal pin surrounded by a circular metal shield. RCA cable and composite cable are interchangeable terms.

Rear Projection Television (RPTV)

A type of television set that uses a rear projection screen in conjunction with red, green, and blue color guns and a series of mirrors to display a video image. Rear projection sets are often called "big screens" due to their large sizes, ranging from 40 to 70 inches in diagonal length. Rear projection television sets can offer incredible pictures, but often require adjustments to obtain optimal picture quality.

Receiver or Home Theater Receiver

A combined signal processor, tuner, and amplifier that allows the input of multiple audio and video signals, decodes various surround sound formats, and delivers output to speakers. The receiver is the center of the home theater system, providing audio and video switching capabilities. (See Figure G.17.)

Figure G.17
The home theater receiver is the center of the home theater system

Red Push

A condition prevalent in some television sets in which the set displays a higher concentration of shades of red than optimal. Images on television sets that have red push appear overly red, especially noticeable on flesh tones.

Reference Level

A level to which you should set your speakers, so that the loudest volume level your system achieves at peak levels is 105 db. Setting your system to reference level is accomplished by using a decibel meter with a calibration disc.

Resistance

A rating of how difficult it is to move current through a circuit. Lower resistance ratings can lead to higher output levels, but it requires the amplifier to work harder. Most home theater speakers offer an 8 ohm average resistance rating.

Resolution

The number of lines of information that make up an image. The higher the resolution, the more detailed the image appears.

S

S-Video Connection

A type of video connection in which the color information is separated from the brightness information. This increased separation results in an improved picture quality over composite video connections.

Scan Velocity Modulation (SVM)

A common feature of television monitors, SVM speeds up and slows down the drawing of the image on the screen to provide more detailed edges. Although this feature is often promoted by manufacturers as a plus, most video enthusiasts agree that it should be disabled to obtain a properly calibrated television set.

SDTV

An acronym for Standard Definition Television, which is a video format that offers 480 lines of interlaced scan resolution.

Sealed Enclosure

A speaker enclosure that is completely sealed and has no port tubes. Sealed enclosures are not as loud as ported enclosures and require more power, but they can offer increased accuracy in reproduction.

Sensitivity Rating

A measure of volume output, rated in decibels, that a speaker produces when given 1 watt of power. A higher sensitivity rating means the speaker can produce a higher volume level when given the same amount of power. By using a speaker with a higher sensitivity rating, you can achieve the same level of volume output without pushing your amplifier as hard. A good sensitivity rating is 89 decibels and above.

Set Top Box (STB)

A common term given to high-definition television tuners. A STB is used to decode a digital, high-definition television signal for display on your television monitor.

Simulated Surround Sound

A method of trying to create a sense of sounds surrounding the viewer using only two speakers. Many television sets offer simulated surround sound modes. These modes are generally not high quality and leave much to be desired.

Sound Pressure Level (SPL)

A measurement, in decibels, of how much pressure is being placed on the ear, which equates to loudness.

Stereo

A recording that has two channels of sound.

Subwoofer

A limited frequency range speaker that re-creates only low-frequency sounds, usually those below 80 Hz. A powered subwoofer is a subwoofer that has its own amplifier to power the subwoofer. Subwoofers are responsible for creating the room-shaking sounds that make movies seem real.

Surround Sound

A term used to describe an audio system that physically surrounds the listener with speakers that send sound waves from all directions. The generic term is often misused by people referring to a Dolby Digital output.

T

THX

The specifications set by Lucasfilms that ensures home theater components meet stringent criteria for performance. Products that are THX certified are considered to be of the highest quality, but they often carry high prices.

THX Certified

A certification given to devices that have met the stringent quality requirements set by Lucasfilm.

Timbre Matching

A process of using front-left and front-right speakers that have the same tonal characteristics as the center channel. When using front speakers that are properly timbre matched, transitions effects are seamless between the three speakers. Most speaker manufacturers sell center channels that match the timbre characteristics of the left and right speakers they sell. Timbre matching the front three speakers is essential.

Time Shifting

The ability to record a television program with a Personal Video Recorder (PVR) and watch it at your convenience. Time shifting includes the ability to pause live television and begin playback at your leisure. PVRs begin recording as soon as you tune to a channel, which allows you to rewind at any point.

Torch Mode

A slang term describing the output of most television sets using the factory default settings. Torch mode refers to the overly high settings of brightness that lead to an incredibly bright picture. Proper calibration of the video monitor corrects this condition. Torch mode can be dangerous to your television set because the increased brightness makes the television set more susceptible to burn in.

Toslink

A term for a digital optical cable. Toslink cables are used to transmit digital signals from devices. Toslink cables use fiber optic technology to send the digital signals. A common use of a toslink cable is to transmit the Dolby Digital or DTS digital bitstream from a DVD player to a home theater receiver.

Total Harmonic Distortion (THD)

The amount of distortion present during playback at a specified output level. Home theater receivers feature power ratings that list the amount of total harmonic distortion present at the given output level. For example, 90 watts x 5 channels at 8 ohms (20 Hz–20 kHz) at .05% THD.

Touch Screen

A screen that responds to touches. The touch then triggers an action from the device. A common example of a touch screen is the Philip's Pronto remote control.

APPENDIX C

Tower Speaker

A speaker that doesn't require the use of a stand to bring the drivers to ear level. Tower speakers usually consist of several drivers and feature a lower frequency response than bookshelf speakers. (See Figure G.18.)

Figure G.18
Tower speakers offer
better bass response
than bookshelf speakers

Treble

The high-frequency sound waves that are usually re-created by the tweeter component of a speaker.

Tweak

The process of performing small adjustments to a component to obtain improved results.

Tweeter

A component of a speaker that reproduces high-frequency signals. The typical frequency response for a tweeter is from 3 kHz to 20 kHz.

U

Universal Remote Control

A remote control that allows the operation of several components. Universal remote controls typically contain a series of preprogrammed codes that tell the remote which infrared commands should be sent for each button pushed. Good universal remote controls also feature learning ability and the ability to record macro commands. (See Figure G.19.)

Figure G.19
Universal remote
controls help you take
command of your home
theater system with a
single remote control

Up Conversion

The process of adding information to a signal. For example, some home theater receivers up convert a composite video signal to an S-Video signal. Up converted video does not have the same quality as a video that originated at the resulting resolution. For example, many HDTVs up convert standard 480i cable sources to 480p by doubling every line. This up converted 480p image is not the same quality as an image that is natively 480p.

V

Video Cassette Recorder (VCR)

A device that uses cassette tapes to record television programming.

Video Shielding

The lining on the inside of the speaker enclosure that keeps the magnetic field created by the speaker's magnet from distorting the picture on your television set. Video shielding is very important for home theater speakers, especially the center channel, because the speakers are usually placed in close proximity to the television monitor.

Voice Matched

Another name for timbre matching.

W

Wide-screen

A term describing a screen that has a wider aspect ratio than the standard 4:3 width to height aspect ratio. A wide-screen television has an aspect ratio of 16:9.

Woofer

The component of a speaker that reproduces low frequencies.

APPENDIX C

Index